SMITHSONIAN MISCELLANEOUS COLLECTIONS
VOLUME 107, NUMBER 12

THE WINELAND VOYAGES

BY

JOHN R. SWANTON

Collaborator, Bureau of American Ethnology

(PUBLICATION 3906)

CITY OF WASHINGTON
PUBLISHED BY THE SMITHSONIAN INSTITUTION
DECEMBER 15, 1947

The Lord Baltimore Press
BALTIMORE, MD., U. S. A.

THE WINELAND VOYAGES

By JOHN R. SWANTON

Collaborator, Bureau of American Ethnology

INTRODUCTION

The narratives of the Wineland (Vinland) voyages occupy, in English translation, only 61 pages in the volume of "Original Narratives of Early American History" dealing with "The Northmen, Columbus, and Cabot," and the actual material on which studies of the voyages themselves and attempts to identify the landing places must be based is of course very much smaller. In the Saga of Eric the Red 6 lines are devoted to Leif's discovery, 10 pages to Karlsefni's voyage. From the Flat Island Book not more than 18 pages are given to all the voyages.[1] On this narrow basis vast structures of theory have been erected and by it an enormous literature has been created. The first appearance of this problem is thus described by Steensby (1918, pp. 18, 19):

Whilst, in the middle ages in the North, it was not doubted that a Wineland existed which had been visited by Icelanders, this information had great difficulty in taking root and maintaining itself in the literary circles of Europe. Even Adam of Bremen found it necessary to state that he had got his knowledge concerning Wineland "not through a fabulous tale, but through reliable accounts from the Danes." It seemed to be a somewhat incredible thought that an island with vines and self-sowing corn should lie on the other side of Greenland with all its ice and cold.

The knowledge of Wineland therefore died out, and the records about it were practically forgotten for several centuries. It was only in the 17th century that the name Wineland was once more drawn into literature, and it was Thermod Torfæus who first, in 1705, through his treatise "Vinlandia," really seriously drew the attention of the literary world to the Norsemen's ancient discovery of America. Finally, in 1837, C. C. Rafn's *Antiquitates Americanae*

---

[1] Throughout this paper I have used the Reeves translations of the Norse documents as given in the volume of "Original Narratives of Early American History" devoted to "The Northmen, Columbus, and Cabot, 985-1503," edited by Julius E. Olson, pages 14-66. This is recognized as one of the best. The material covers such a small space that it is considered unnecessary to refer to the particular page that is being quoted.

came out, and gave the literary world a summary of the Icelandic accounts of the Wineland voyages.

Rafn also attempted to identify those points on the North American coast at which the Norse voyagers had touched. From this time on the voyages were mentioned in all works dealing with the history of America or the territories along its northeastern seaboard, and Rafn's conclusions were widely accepted until a critical examination of the sources was undertaken by Gustav Storm, whose work appeared in 1887. Shortly afterward, in 1890, the narratives were made available to English and American scholars in the original and in translation by Arthur M. Reeves, along with the results of Storm's investigations.

There are three principal original documents describing the Wineland voyages, but two of these differ only in details and are regarded as essentially one narrative to which the name of the Saga of Eric the Red has usually been given, although the real hero of the story is Thorfinn Karlsefni, and its heroine his wife Gudrid. The third document is a compilation called usually the Flatey Book or Flat Island Book, the preparation of which dates from a somewhat later period. Storm's researches resulted in establishing to the satisfaction of most scholars the vastly greater reliability of the Saga, thereby reversing the attitude which, following Rafn, had hitherto prevailed. This conclusion was not always accepted, however, and in particular a Danish naval officer, William Hovgaard, in a work entitled "The Voyages of the Norsemen to America" (1915), maintained that the two narratives were of equal value. He was promptly answered by Finnur Jónsson, and Storm and Jónsson have been followed by all the more careful students of the Wineland expeditions. Their attempts to determine what points on the American main were visited by Leif and Karlsefni have been based upon the Saga to the practical exclusion of the story in the Flat Island Book. Storm's conclusions are undoubtedly justified as giving a judicious appraisement of the relative value of the two sources, yet I submit that adverse criticism may be overdone. A hostile critic might work as much havoc with the Saga as others have with the story of the Greenlanders, and in my study of the voyages which follows I have tried to weigh the value of the two sources as justly as possible.

If one of two documents dealing with certain historical events is taken as an infallible guide and everything which diverges from it is rejected, the truth may be obscured although the document chosen is the better of the two. In the present instance I hold that students are right in placing the Saga of Eric the Red in the primary position, but it does not therefore follow that it is invariably correct and the Flat Island Book always in error. Essentially the Saga is the story of Thorfinn Karlsefni and his American expedition; it is based, I feel, on the reports of eyewitnesses on an actual voyage, and I am inclined to give great weight to the statements it contains. It is disappointing, however, in the small space devoted to other expeditions, and I am of the opinion that the Flat Island Book has preserved certain items regarding them which had escaped the writer of the Saga. I do not think that its account of Karlsefni's expedition is merely a garbled version of that contained in the Saga. In the discussion to follow we shall try to see what it seems possible to make out of these narratives by a careful cross-examination and the demands of logic.

Following upon Gustav Storm's work, the wave of enthusiasm for "precursers of Columbus" and for things Scandinavian gave place to a counter wave of skepticism. In 1892 J. P. McLean, in order to confute the claims being put forth that many Atlantic crossings had been made before Columbus and that Columbus had learned of America through the Norsemen, attacked with vigor and success various stories of trans-Atlantic voyages by Irish, Welsh, and others, but pressed his charges also against the claims of the Icelanders and Greenlanders. This is reflected in the writings of the period by less extreme opponents. In the same year B. H. DuBois wrote: "That the Northmen sailed south along the coast of America is not improbable, but it *cannot be proved*." A similar opinion rendered by a committee of the Massachusetts Historical Society (1887) has often been quoted and well exemplifies the attitude toward this question by the scholars of the period (McLean, 1892, p. 39):

There is the same sort of reason for believing in the existence of Leif Ericson that there is for believing in the existence of Agamemnon—they are both traditions accepted by later writers; but there is no more reason for regarding as true the details related about his discoveries than there is for accepting as historic truth the narratives contained in the Homeric poems. It is antecedently probable that the Northmen discovered America in the early part of the eleventh century; and this discovery is confirmed by the same sort of historical tradition, not strong enough to be called evidence, upon which our belief in many of the accepted facts of history rests.

Skepticism reached its culmination, however, in Fridtjof Nansen's work "In Northern Mists" (1911), which cast doubt upon the historicity of all of the Wineland narratives though Nansen did not deny that the Norsemen had some knowledge of the coasts west and southwest of Davis Strait. However, Nansen has had few followers and in the light of the researches of northern scholars among early documents and archeological investigations of the Norse ruins in Greenland, Leif and Karlsefni can no longer be classed with Agamemnon. That they were historical characters cannot reasonably be doubted, whereas, in spite of the tablets of Boghaz Koi, Agamemnon remains in the domain of legend. The factual basis of the stories of the Norse voyagers is tacitly admitted by later students in devoting their attention almost entirely to studies of the locations which they visited, though depending mainly, almost uniformly in fact, upon the Saga of Eric the Red. Notable among later studies are those of H. P. Steensby, Finnur Jónsson, W. H. Babcock, Juul Dieserud, William Hovgaard, Halldór Hermannsson, and Matthias Thórdarson.

In addition to the above and to a number of scholarly publications besides, there has been an exceptional output of uncritical literature attempting to place Leif and his successors in all possible and impossible places, and to trace certain remains to them, some of it, like the works of Prof. E. N. Horsford, elaborately and expensively clothed. The fact of the matter is that the data are just strong enough to tempt one to theorize and just weak enough to open the door for an immense amount of speculation, especially if one has an undisciplined imagination and a plentiful supply of local pride or wishful thinking. In pursuit of their investigations students have emphasized or questioned almost every statement of the narratives, picked up the slightest hint, attempted to read the minds of the explorers and chroniclers, and frequently to read into their minds things which never occurred to them. Charts of the entire northeastern coast of America have been microscopically examined, the fauna and flora in its present distribution and possible past distribution haled into court, and the precise meaning of this, that, and the other Icelandic word discussed at length. It is one of those investigations which enable men who pride themselves on their acumen to prove it by leaving the problems ostentatiously alone or by registering skepticism, the cheapest way there is to acquire a reputation for scientific ability.

Yet, after all has been said, we may remark that—as with philosophies—while all Wineland theories have been partly wrong, they have not been entirely wrong. And it is but fair to add that some progress has been made and that, although we are not optimistic enough to believe, like Horsford, that we can determine where Leif and Karlsefni came ashore near enough to erect monuments, we can determine areas within which beyond reasonable doubt the landings took place. We must deal with areas instead of points and probabilities instead of absolutes.

I have been attracted to this problem in part by my studies of the Indian tribes of North America, and in part by my experience in attempting to extract the truth out of a number of conflicting narratives dealing with explorations in other parts of the New World. An examination of the two sources leads me to think that we have here a problem somewhat similar to one that I have faced twice before—in French and in Spanish. Beside the well-documented, historical narratives covering early colonial times in Louisiana we have a pseudo-historical work by the engineer Pénicaut, the chronology of which is utterly misleading and the record of events seriously disjointed and often garbled. The chronicles of the De Soto expedition present us with something similar. Here we have three narratives which are very nearly factual in their statements and a fourth which is highly elaborated, verbose, frequently inaccurate as to dates and the sequence of events, and teeming with exaggerations. Yet Pénicaut and Garcilaso de la Vega have preserved certain matters of distinct value to us overlooked by the other chroniclers. As an example I might cite Garcilaso's elaborate accounts of two expeditions sent from the Indian town of Cofitachequi to apprehend a chieftainess of that place. As two of our most reliable authorities ignore these completely, it seemed at first as if the stories of them might be wholly apochryphal. Until, that is, upon turning to the third and briefest narrative, we read that the chieftainess in question left her town suddenly and that De Soto "caused her to be sought." Therefore, when we have a narrative of this type, such as seems to be contained in the Flat Island Book, it is fair to give it careful examination and not to dismiss it cavalierly under a blanket indictment covering the document in which it is contained. As a result of my own examination I conclude that, while the strictures of Storm and his successors, aside from those based on linguistic grounds which I am not equipped to discuss, are in large measure justified, the condemnation has frequently been too sweeping, and on the other hand the Saga of Eric the Red will not stand up much better under the same sort of criticism.

As just intimated, the writer is not conversant with the language in which the Sagas were written or the related tongues, but this side of the question has been so carefully covered by others that it is pretty safe to take one's information second-hand. These preliminaries having been disposed of, let us proceed to a study of the story which the narratives under discussion reveal.

STORY OF THE EXPEDITIONS

In the year 982 Eric the Red was banished from Iceland for a period of 3 years. About 900 (Fischer says 920) a Norwegian named Gunnbiörn on the way from his own country to Iceland had been blown out of his course, and he discovered some islands to the west which were afterward called Gunnbiörn's Rocks (Brunn, 1918, p. 4; Fischer, 1903, p. 6). Eric directed his course thither, reached the coast of Greenland, and rounding its southernmost point, discovered the more habitable parts on the western coast. When the period of his exile was over, he returned to Iceland with such flattering accounts of the new land that intending colonists flocked back with him—in 25 vessels according to some, 35 according to others (Brunn, 1918, p. 28; Fischer, 1903, p. 20; Olson, 1906, p. 16; Babcock, 1913, p. 34). Only 14 actually arrived, the rest having been lost or forced to return, but more soon followed and two main settlements were formed, the East Settlement about the present Julianehaab and the West Settlement, the smaller of the two, in the Godthaab district. Eric himself settled in a fiord now called Tunugdliarfik which took his name and was known as Ericsfiord, at a place called Brattahlid. The next deep inlet to the south, now Igalikofiord, was known as Einarsfiord, and at Gardar on a neck of land between the two came to be located the Episcopal seat of the Bishop of Greenland. In the small fiord now called Amitsuarsuk a prominent man named Heriulf settled, and the inlet was in consequence known as Heriulfsfiord. The point Ikigeit just north of the entrance was called Heriulfsness. These and numerous other points in the two Greenland settlements have been carefully located by Danish scholars (Brunn, 1918, p. 28).

Eric had three sons, Thorstein, Leif, and Thorvald, the last probably illegitimate, and an illegitimate daughter Freydis, married to a man named Thorvard.

In the summer of 999 Leif voyaged to Norway, where he spent the following winter with King Olaf Tryggvason, and on his departure he was commissioned by the king to carry Christianity to Greenland, a charge which he accepted with some misgivings. Substantially the same story is told by the Saga and the Flat Island Book. Of Leif's return voyage to Greenland the latter says nothing, but according to the former it was during this return voyage that he discovered America.

For a long time he was tossed about upon the ocean, and came upon lands of which he had previously had no knowledge. There were self-sown wheat fields and vines growing there. There were also those trees there which are called "mausur," and of all these they took specimens. Some of the timbers were so large that they were used in building.

The above is in the narrative generally relied upon by students of the Norse voyages, who therefore date the discovery of America in the year 1000. But, whether erroneously or not, the Flat Island Book tells of another and earlier landfall and makes that the inspiration for a later voyage to the new land by Leif. Mention has been made of the prominent Greenland settler named Heriulf and of his settlement in Amitsuarsukfiord. So much is beyond dispute. According to the Flat Island Book, however, this Heriulf had a very promising son Biarni who early evinced a taste for voyaging and finally obtained possession of a trading vessel. "It was his custom," goes the tale, "to pass his winters alternately abroad and with his father," but during the last winter that he spent away, this time at least in Norway, his father accompanied Eric to Greenland.

Biarni arrived with his ship at Eyrar [in Iceland] in the summer of the same year, in the spring of which his father had sailed away. Biarni was much surprised when he heard this news, and would not discharge his cargo. His shipmates inquired of him what he intended to do, and he replied that it was his purpose to keep to his custom, and make his home for the winter with his father; "and I will take the ship to Greenland, if you will bear me company." They all replied that they would abide by his decision. Then said Biarni, "Our voyage must be regarded as foolhardy, seeing that no one of us has ever been in the Greenland sea." Nevertheless they put out to sea when they were equipped for the voyage, and sailed for three days, until the land was hidden by the water, and then the fair wind died out, and north winds arose, and fogs, and they knew not whither they were drifting, and thus it lasted for many "dœgr." Then they saw the sun again, and were able to determine the quarters of the heavens; they hoisted sail, and sailed that "dœgr" through before they saw land.

In brief, they sight three countries in succession before reaching Greenland, and to come upon each new land takes 1 "dœgr" more than the last, 2 to pass from the first to the second, 3 to pass from the second to the third, 4 to pass from the third to Greenland, and finally Biarni comes to land directly in front of his father's house in the last-mentioned country. This narrative has been rejected practically in toto by later writers, and they may be justified in doing so. Although Heriulf is a well-known personage, no son of his named Biarni is otherwise revealed to us. Possibly, as has been suggested, Biarni was a companion of Leif when he voyaged from Norway to Greenland via America, or it may be that the entire tale is but a garbled account of that voyage and Biarni another name for Leif. There is some paral-

8 SMITHSONIAN MISCELLANEOUS COLLECTIONS VOL. 107

lelism it must be admitted. Biarni is tossed about on the ocean in traveling from Iceland to Greenland much as Leif was in going from Norway to the same place. A little later the Flat Island Book tells us that Biarni, like Leif, went to Norway, became acquainted with the then king, Earl Eric, related his travels to that monarch, "was appointed one of the Earl's men, and went out to Greenland the following summer." And finally Biarni's father and Leif's father were near neighbors and lived in adjoining fiords. Although Leif spent more time in America than Biarni, both seem to have been anxious to get home to their parents. The three lands which Biarni saw are uniformly identified with the three that Leif and Thorfinn Karlsefni saw according to the Flat Island Book, which, as we shall see presently, drops one stopping place of Karlsefni out of the picture.

It has also been suggested that Biarni Heriulfson may have derived his existence from the story of Biarni Grimolfsson, who appears in the Saga as a fellow merchant of Karlsefni, like the other Biarni voyaged to Greenland from Iceland, and like him was caught in a storm at sea a little later.

Naturally enough the arithmetical progression by which Biarni Heriulfson reached the several lands he encountered is held up against the historicity of the narrative, as is the reported accuracy with which he ultimately found his father's home, one he had never seen. The "foolhardy" venturesomeness of the expedition into an unknown sea is also urged against it just as Biarni himself is said to have anticipated.

It is only fair, however, to enter some counterarguments. For instance, the stories of Leif's visit to King Olaf and Biarni's to that king's successor are in the same narrative in the Flat Island Book where there is less likelihood of duplication than if they were from different sources. Norse captains voyaged back and forth frequently between Norway, Iceland, and Greenland, and there is no reason why several voyages should not be recorded. Biarni visited three lands on his way to Greenland and landed on none of them. Leif apparently visited but one and he actually landed upon that, bringing back with him specimens of the self-sown wheat, vines, and timber. Heriulf, as well as Eric, was a prominent man, and there is no reason why he should not have had a noteworthy son. The fact that he and Eric lived in neighboring fiords is of minor consequence in its bearings on the movements of their offspring. The resemblance between Biarni Heriulfson and Biarni Grimolfsson is superficial. Both voyaged to Greenland from Iceland, but so did almost all the Greenland colonists. Both went to America, but under very different conditions, the one driven by accident, the other as a companion of Karlsefni on a purposeful voyage. Both were caught in a storm on the ocean, but the experience was too common to have any significance, and while Heriulfson seems to have made his home in Greenland and died peacefully there, Grimolfsson was drowned at sea.

Again, it does not follow, as has been assumed, that the first of the three lands seen by Biarni was identical with Wineland. The third land he came upon before reaching Greenland is known to have been Helluland, for it is distinctly stated, and the identity of the second with Markland, although not stated, is to be inferred rather clearly, but the connection of the first with Wineland is by no means evident. It was "level, and covered with woods," and "there were small hillocks upon it." Only by the "hillocks" does it differ from the description of Markland. What is said later on regarding Wineland by the writers of both narratives does not emphasize the forests particularly, though they are often noted incidentally, and the only approach to a mention of "hillocks" is in the Saga, where it says "wherever there was hilly ground, there were vines." This is a rather slender thread to hang an identification upon. The two wooded lands might have been Newfoundland and southern Labrador or Newfoundland and Nova Scotia.

Another point may be added in connection with Helluland. If the two narratives were taken from the same source, we should expect a closer resemblance between the descriptions of that country. The Saga says of it: "They .... found there large flat stones (*hellur*) and many of these were twelve ells wide." According to the Biarni narrative, however, "this land was high and mountainous, with ice-mountains upon it," and later, in describing Leif's supposed visit to the same country, the Flat Island Book says they "saw no grass there; great ice mountains lay inland back from the sea, and it was as a (tableland) of flat rock all the way from the sea to the ice mountains." One further point may be significant. When Biarni and his fellow voyagers turned their prow away from Helluland and filled away for Greenland, the chronicler says that they "saw that it was an island." This is an incident of which there was no particular need in a made-up narrative, and it is improbable that this island has any connection with the Biarney Island or Islands that Karlsefni sailed past when he crossed from Greenland to Helluland.

The intervals of 1, 2, 3, and 4 "dœgr" in making the passages from land to land is admittedly highly suspicious, but so is the use of 2 "dœgr" two or three times in succession in the Saga of Eric the Red.

Mythic formulas of this kind may be introduced into narratives without altogether destroying their historicity.

The Biarni narrative has been condemned for very opposite reasons—because of Biarni's alleged attempt to reach Greenland which neither he nor any of his men had seen, and because of the assertion that he was driven so far out of his course. It will be noticed that he himself anticipated the first criticism. But Greenland is only about 200 miles from Iceland, and the direction in which it lay was well known. Biarni's venture seems to me no more foolhardy than that of Thorstein Ericsson, who set out to cross Davis Strait to a land visited but once before by any Norseman, or that of Thorhall in sailing for Greenland from Streamfirth with a crew of nine men, or more particularly the voyages of Leif from Greenland to Norway and return, but of those more presently. As to the second, it should be recalled that when Greenland was settled, of 25 or 35 vessels setting out from Iceland only 14 arrived in spite of the fact that they were guided by Eric. Also that Thorbiorn and his friends in attempting the same passage experienced "great gales," "lost their way," and did not arrive until "the very eve of winter." Thorstein's failure to reach his objective, which some of his men had visited, was much more monumental than that of Biarni to arrive at once in Greenland, where no one on his ship had been. Yet these adventures are all described in the supposedly authentic Saga of Eric the Red. As to the distances to which Thorstein and Biarni were driven, there is not much to choose between them if Biarni actually reached the New England coast, which there is reason to doubt, and Thorstein, who knew presumably where he was going, deserves more blame for his failure than Biarni who merely had the general direction. However, as we have already seen, it is not necessary to imagine that Biarni went so far. If Biarni's voyage is "incredible," Thorstein's is still more so.

It is also held up against the Biarni narrative that its hero is made to come upon the coast of Greenland exactly in front of his father's home which neither he nor any of his crew had visited. This may very well be an item in the build-up of his hero by the compiler of the tale. Still, accidents of the kind have happened, and it may be mentioned as a possible explanation that Heriulfsness lay "below" two high mountains called Hvidserk and Hvarf, the latter a landmark for vessels voyaging between Greenland and Iceland or Greenland and Norway, and that near it was a harbor called Sand "which was a universal harbor for Norwegians and merchants." There is still less reason for criticizing the Flat Island Book because it represents later voyagers to Wineland as having reached without difficulty the cabins Leif had erected there. If one is to be literalistic he might cavil at the Saga for saying that "Leif landed in Ericsfirth" on his return from Wineland as too specific, and that is the only landfall given for Thorstein after he had tossed about on the ocean all summer. Nor does Karlsefni seem to have had any difficulty in reentering Streamfirth on his return from Wineland. Must one supply complete logbooks of all the Norse voyages?

Equally unreasonable is the attack on the Flat Island Book chronicle because it says that Biarni settled in Greenland and "gave up his voyaging," yet proceeds immediately afterward to relate a visit he made to the court of the King of Norway. The sentence on which this criticism is based runs as follows: "Biarni now went to his father, gave up his voyaging, and remained with his father while Heriulf lived, and continued to live there after his father." Now, the "voyaging" that he gave up was plainly his annual trading expeditions, and it is not said that he "continued to live" at Heriulfsness until his death. He made his home there, but the wording does not exclude visits to other countries.

My experience with narratives of this kind has taught me that, while corruptions and confusions are common, absolute fictions are rare and usually of a kind to be identified with comparative ease. I am inclined to think, therefore, that there is something other than pure fiction behind this story of Biarni. Iceland lay nearer the American main than Norway, and if we can believe that Leif came to America from Norway across the entire breadth of the North Atlantic, its discovery by a voyager from Iceland does not seem incredible. We may well doubt the time scale assigned to him and the accuracy of his Greenland landfall, as reported, and marvel at his seeming want of curiosity regarding the lands he observed, but we must not expect too much of chroniclers of the fourteenth and fifteenth centuries, and on the last point recollect that the summer was far advanced and voyaging on the northern seas in winter greatly dreaded.

I would give up Biarni more readily were it not that the story of Leif's voyage contained in the supposedly more reliable Saga of Eric the Red is almost as amazing, in some ways even more so. If Biarni was blown out of his way as far as the New England coast, he covered about 2,400 statute miles, but it is not necessary to suppose that he got farther than Newfoundland, a voyage of about 1,600 miles, whereas Leif apparently crossed the full breadth of the North Atlantic nonstop, and even if we suppose he did not get farther than Nova Scotia, that means a voyage of about 3,000 miles out of sight of land, close to Columbus' record, and what a difference in the size of vessels and in the weather! As sometimes charted, this would have been against the flow of the Gulf Stream and in the teeth of the prevailing winds. To make his voyage at all credible we must suppose that he kept well to the north, taking advantage of the counter current past Iceland and around the southern point of Greenland and the easterly winds in that latitude, and was caught by a north wind off Greenland. From Iceland on, this is the course that must be assumed for Biarni. The sailing directions from Norway to Greenland are thus given by Brunn (1918, legend, pl. 6):

Leaving Hernum (islands near Bergen) going towards the west to Hvarf in Greenland [identified by him with Nunarssuit (Cape Desolation)] . . . . ; as one goes north round Hjatland ([S]Hetland), one could just see the land, thereafter south round the Fâeroe islands, so that one saw half the height of the mountains, to the south round Iceland, so that the sea birds and whales could be seen (in one place the distance is given as 48 miles), after which one came to the high land in Greenland, which is called Hvarf. The day before, another high mountain is seen, which is called Hvidserk (in the vicinity of Greenland's southernmost point), and below (between?) these two mountains - - - Heriolfsness lies, and near to it is a harbour, which is called Sand, which was a universal harbour for Norwegians and merchants.

The sailing directions from Iceland to the Eastern Settlement of Greenland, indicating the course which Biarni should have taken, were as follows (ibid.):

a) The ancient course: From Snæfellsness, two days and two nights sailing straight to the west to Gunbiørns skerries, midway between Greenland and Iceland (i.e., one had traversed half the way to the eastern settlement. Gunbiørns skerries most likely lay in the present Angmagssalik on Greenland's east coast beneath 66° n. lat.). b) The later course, after ice having come "out of the sea bays" so near to the skerries, that no one could sail the ancient direction without danger of life: From Snæfellsness straight to the west for one day and one night, just slightly to south west so as to escape the above mentioned ice, which lies near Gunbiørns skerries, and then on for one day and one night to the north west, then one comes under Hvarf. From Snæfellsness, the shortest way to Greenland is "four days sailing" (Landnáma).

If we accept the story of Leif's voyage as given in the Saga, we must suppose that he was carried along this northern route, without seeing Iceland or Greenland apparently, and was then caught in a north wind and carried to America. An amazing trip at that. Biarni's adventure is less incredible, especially if we assume that he was not carried farther south than Newfoundland, and when we compare the two, we are led to the suspicion that the story of Leif's voyage in the

Saga leaves something out, and that the discovery was actually due to an independent voyage inspired by Biarni's accidental discovery. In either case we may still regard Leif as the discoverer of Wineland. I think, too, that the writer of the narrative in the Flat Island Book has confused the stories of Leif's and Karlsefni's visits to Wineland.

These points are raised, not to destroy faith in the Saga as our most reliable source of information regarding the Wineland voyages, but in order to light up a tendency to allow a belief, however well founded, to become a dogma and warp one's critical faculty. Thus Leif's voyage across the entire width of the North Atlantic is said to be "probable" because incorporated into the narrative of a preferred authority, while Biarni's is "improbable" or even "impossible" because the document containing it has been condemned.

But why did not the Greenlanders take more interest in Biarni's discoveries until Leif's return from Norway 14 years later? However, one might have asked, Why did not the Icelanders take more interest in Gunnbiörn's Rocks until more than 60 years had passed? Probably for the same reason. When Gunnbiörn made his discovery, Iceland had not been completely occupied and the population had not begun to press upon the available supply of land. When Biarni discovered America—if he did—all that he observed of the country was that toward the south it was wooded and the wooded land lay at a distance with a region of desolation (Helluland) in between. Greenland was just being settled, the good sites were not all taken up, and the more readily available supplies of wood had not been exhausted.

But, according to the Saga, this lack of enterprise was shared in even greater degree by Leif, for after having landed in Wineland, and having obtained samples of "self-sown wheat," vines, and "mausur" wood, he returned with them to Greenland without displaying the least personal ambition to visit that land of riches again. Thus, in six lines, the Saga tells us that Leif made one of the greatest discoveries of all time, and noted and sampled the principal riches of the country as described by all later visitors. On his way back he rescued some people from a wreck, took them home with him, and procured quarters for them during the winter. "In this wise," the narrative proceeds, "he showed his nobleness and goodness, since he introduced Christianity into the country, and saved the men from the wreck; and he was called Leif the Lucky ever after"—"Lucky," not because he discovered a continent more than four times as big as Europe, but because he rescued some men at sea and introduced a new religion into Greenland. Here is a man, if we are to trust the Saga, with a soul above skittles, and, more remarkable still, he is the son of that same man who brought about a mass migration to the second largest block of ice in the world by naming it Greenland. How the old man must have fumed at this degenerate son of his who spent his time caring for shipwrecked mariners and spreading the gospel of a spiritual world instead of becoming the father of a great material one! That helps to explain Eric's stubborn adherence to paganism. He belonged to the Order of the Main Chance. If the Saga is correct, Leif did not even take enough interest in his Land of Wine to visit it a second time. Except for his affair with the woman Thorgunna in the Hebrides, he would deserve sainthood and, as one who preferred "Greenland's icy mountains" to the fertile empire of Yankee-dom, he would naturally become Greenland's patron saint. As things are, he should stand second only to Eric in the affections of Greenlanders and have his own monument in Ericsdall.

However, when we remember that Biarni Heriulfson would not even land in America because he was anxious to get home to his father, we have to admit that these rugged Northmen had virtues to put us to shame. We have credited them overmuch with a lust for rapine and skull cracking, but here are two glittering exceptions, a man who to the riches of America prefers rescuing mariners and preaching religion, and another who turns all mainland America down in favor of his father.

Speaking more seriously, however, does not this visit of Leif to Wineland after a nonstop passage of the entire North Atlantic, cavalier dismissal of the whole experience, and subsequent utter indifference, seem a bit fishy even when told by our "most reliable" authority? Or does it mean that Karlsefni had the better press agent? Upon the whole does it not seem rather probable that Leif should have made an extended visit to Wineland, whether from the suggestion of a previous explorer or an earlier chance landfall by himself?

We will consider Leif's supposed expedition from Greenland later, but there is one item which apparently must be assigned to it or else to his landfall in a voyage from Norway as the Saga has it. That is the story of the discovery of grapes, of which we have two versions. The one contained in the Saga places the event at Streamfirth considerably north of the true Wineland and gives it as an event in the voyage of Karlsefni, but it has long been recognized that this is an interpolation and it is almost universally held that Streamfirth was well north of the land of grapes. According to this story the discovery was made by two Gaels named Haki and Hækia who were very fleet of foot and had been presented to Leif by King Olaf and by him loaned to Karlsefni. These two were set on land at a point near the mouth of Streamfirth and told to run south to view the country and return before the end of the third half-day. When they came back, one had a bunch of grapes and the other an ear of new-sown wheat.

According to the Flat Island Book grapes were discovered during Leif's stay in Wineland when he reached that country from Greenland, and by a German named Tyrker who had long been in Eric's family and was regarded by Leif as a foster father. The narrative states that on arriving in Wineland, the Norsemen put up a substantial house, and after that Leif began a systematic exploration, half of his people going out to examine the country each day and half remaining at home, the parties alternating in exploration and housekeeping. The explorers were directed not to go beyond points from which they could return the same day. One evening Tyrker was missing but when search was made he soon appeared in a highly excited state of mind reporting the discovery of grapes. Forthwith Leif directed his people to begin loading their vessel with vines, grapes, and wood for the return journey "and when spring came they sailed away."

The very name given to this country shows that to the adventurers the most striking thing about it was the presence of grapes, and that is why these two stories have been preserved—or concocted. Except for the use subsequently made of this fruit, there is not much to choose between the two narratives on the ground of credibility. It is possible that there is a connection between the names of Hækia (of which Haki seems to be a synonym) and Tyrker, but the two Gaelic runners suggest to me more that they may be products of mythic lore than does the appearance of a German. I am not informed as to the status of grapes in Scotland or Ireland and the early use of wine there, but the story of the German appears the more probable. Hermannsson (1936, p. 38) unjustifiably interprets this man's excitement as due to intoxication. The narrative suggests only elation at his find and the possibilities it involved. The point in this narrative about which one may well feel skeptical is the preservation of a load of grapes all winter and their transportation in usable shape to Greenland, unless, that is, we suppose them to have been carefully dried. The Saga merely says that Leif took specimens of the vines he found in Wineland without indicating whether there were grapes attached and if so in what shape they reached their destination. It notes the fact that Karlsefni found vines in Wineland but says not a word of any use to which their fruit was put by him. According to the Flat Island Book, however, quantities were brought back by every explorer. Here apparently the reputation of the country has overbalanced the chronicler's judgment. At the same time he should be cleared of a false accusation to the effect that he describes grape gathering as taking place in the spring. The translation runs: "A cargo sufficient for the ship was cut, and when the spring came, they made their ship ready, and sailed away."

If there is any truth in either of the stories of how grapes were found as above given, they belong to Leif's explorations and not to Karlsefni's. The attempt to find in Tyrker a distorted version of Thorhall the Huntsman appears to me far-fetched. Except that both are said to have lived with Eric, I find no resemblance between them whatever.

On his way back from Wineland to Greenland, according to both of our narratives, Leif rescued some people who had been shipwrecked and brought them to Greenland to spend the winter with him. The Saga places this event, of course, at the end of his voyage from Norway, but the other during his return from a special voyage to Wineland. The Flat Island Book has confounded the voyage of Thorbiorn and his daughter Gudrid from Iceland to Greenland with the story of this wreck, probably because the hospitality of Eric was extended to both parties involved and they arrived about the same time. Holand (1940, p. 29) has supplied a satisfactory explanation of the confusion by calling attention to the fact that another Gudrid, "the daughter of one Ingjald in Iceland, went to Norway where she married and about this time came to Greenland."

According to the Flat Island Book, Leif's brother Thorvald voyaged to Wineland after Leif returned, but the next expedition detailed by the Saga was led by another brother, Thorstein, who is highly praised. The explorers urged Eric to accompany them believing that it would bring them luck, and though the old man demurred, he finally consented. Before setting out he carefully hid a little chest containing gold and silver, but on his way to the vessel the horse on which he was riding threw him, "broke his ribs and dislocated his shoulder," and he attributed this accident to the fact that he had hidden his treasure and therefore he sent word to his wife to go and get it. He was not, however, deterred from accompanying the explorers, but they had a very stormy voyage and were driven in sight of Iceland "and likewise saw birds from the Irish coast." "In the autumn they turned back, worn out by toil, and exposure to the elements, and exhausted by their labors, and arrived at Ericsfirth at the very beginning of winter." All those not otherwise provided for were cared for at Brattahlid during that winter.

The Flat Island Book describes this attempted visit to Wineland in much the same language but with certain important changes. The effort to have Eric as a companion is placed not at the beginning of this trip but before that of Leif already mentioned. As in the other narrative, Eric finally consents and rides to the boat and, as in that, he is thrown from his horse. However, it is his foot which is hurt, nothing is said of any concealed treasure, and he gives up and returns home. Thorstein's object in making the voyage, according to the same document, was to bring home the body of his brother Thorvald. This desire loses some of the "strangeness" which has been charged against it when we remember how insistent Thorstein himself was, after his own death, that his body and the bodies of his companions with one exception be removed from Lysufirth for burial in consecrated ground. It comes out prominently in both sagas. According to the Flat Island Book, Thorstein marries Gudrid before putting to sea and takes her with him, whereas, according to the Saga, he did not marry her until after his return. Again, instead of returning to Ericsfirth and moving afterward to Lysufirth for the winter, the Flat Island Book takes him directly to Lysufirth. In these particulars it is probable that the Saga is more nearly correct.

In reporting the attempt to take Eric along, on the other hand, the narrative given in the Flat Island Book seems more probable and I therefore follow it and assume that it belongs to the expedition of Leif. The Saga reports that on the morning of his departure Eric concealed his gold and silver, and the reason for this is not apparent since his wife remained at home and his house was presumably occupied by responsible persons during his absence. It may have been because his wife had offended him, but I do not understand that gold and silver figured much in Greenland trade at that period. What the farmers did not raise themselves they got by barter. Nor is it likely that Eric's wife would abscond from the best farm in Greenland, there being no place to abscond to within any reasonable distance and no ready means of transportation. But the incredible part of the story is the assertion that, after being thrown from his horse and having some ribs broken and a shoulder dislocated, Eric was not deterred from venturing out upon the boisterous waves of the North Atlantic. If so, he was a remarkably tough specimen. No doubt the Norse had a rough and ready method of treating dislocated shoulders, but one wonders what they did about the broken ribs, and if Eric partook of those "high spirits" with which, as the chronicler assures us, they all set out. According to the Flat Island Book, however, in falling from his horse Eric merely wounded his foot and yet he gave up his intention to go to sea and returned home.

The two narratives are in substantial agreement as to the size of the crew which Thorstein had and their trials.

Thorstein and Gudrid spent the next winter at Lysufirth and the remarkable events which took place there are detailed at length by both of our chroniclers. As just stated, they differ as to the time when Thorstein and Gudrid were married and the time when they went to Lysufirth. The Saga states that they removed because Thorstein owned an estate there jointly with another Thorstein called Thorstein the Swarthy. According to the Flat Island Book they landed at Lysufirth and were unable to find lodgings for the winter until the other Thorstein took them in. The narratives agree, however, in saying that Thorstein Ericsson and the wife of Thorstein the Swarthy died that winter, that the corpses of both came to life afterward, and that Thorstein Ericsson then informed Gudrid that she was to marry an Icelander and have illustrious progeny. However, they differ in enough details to show that we have separate streams of tradition. According to the Saga, Thorstein the Swarthy's wife was named Sigrid; according to the other document it was Grimhild. The Saga alone tells us that she saw the spirits of her dead companions and of herself as a prelude to her own death, and that the principal among them was the overseer of the estate, Gard, who was responsible for the various apparitions. In consequence Thorstein instructs his wife that Gard's body is to be burned but that the others must be taken to Ericsfirth to be buried in consecrated ground. In the Flat Island Book Thorstein is made to foretell to his wife not merely her marriage to an Icelander but a later pilgrimage to "the South," that is, to Rome, and that she will finally take the veil. Both agree as to the final disposition of the bodies and also in stating that Gudrid went to live at Brattahlid, though the Saga informs us that she stayed with Eric, while the Flat Island Book says Leif, having previously entered a note to the effect that Eric was dead. In this last item the Saga appears to have been correct.

At this point Thorfinn Karlsefni, the central figure of the Saga and the most important one in the Flat Island Book, comes upon the scene from Iceland. His ancestry is given with considerable care by both chroniclers. It seems that he was a successful trader, and one summer, the summer of 1002 apparently, he equipped his ship for a voyage to Greenland accompanied by a man named Snorri, Thorbriand's son, of Alptafirth. In a second vessel having the same destination sailed Biarni, Grimolf's son, a man from Breidafirth, and Thorhall, an East-firth man. They landed in Ericsfirth, drove a brisk trade that autumn and, at Eric's invitation, spent the winter with him. During that winter Gudrid and Karlesfni were married. Regarding these events the two narratives are in accord.

"About this time," runs the Saga, "there began to be much talk at Brattahlid, to the effect that Wineland the Good should be explored, for, it was said, that country must be possessed of many good qualities." Karlsefni and the other commanders of the two Icelandic vessels agreed to go thither, and a third vessel was added, manned by Greenlanders from Ericsfirth, among whom were Eric's son Thorvald, his daughter Freydis, her husband Thorvard, and a man named Thorvall the Huntsman who "had been for a long time with Eric as his hunter and fisherman during the summer, and as his steward during the winter." "He was a poor Christian," the Saga continues, but "had a wide knowledge of the unsettled regions," which would be those along the northwest Greenland coast. They sailed in the ship Thorbiorn had brought out, according to the same authority, and 160 men went along, besides cattle. Although the Flat Island Book mentions only one vessel in which went 60 men and 5 women, it adds, "they took with them all kinds of cattle, as it was their intention to settle the country, if they could." One wonders how many kinds of cattle could be accommodated in one vessel besides the 65 human beings.

When Karlsefni and his companions set out upon this voyage—

they sailed to the Western Settlement, and thence to Bear Island (or the Bear Islands). From that point they bore away to the southward for two dœgr. Then they saw land and launched a boat, and explored the land, and found there large flat stones (*hellur*), and many of these were twelve ells wide; there were many Arctic foxes there. They gave a name to the country, and called it Helluland (the land of flat stones).

The several landfalls of Karlsefni between Greenland and Wineland are not mentioned in the Flat Island Book, having already been described in the accounts it gives of the supposed voyages of Biarni from south to north and Leif from north to south. Neither of these is said to have touched the Western Settlement, and there is no note of Bear Island unless it could be identical with the Helluland Island in the account of Biarni's expedition. The descriptions of Helluland in the Saga and in the Flat Island Book have been compared already.

The Saga story of Karlsefni's voyage now continues as follows:

Then they sailed with northerly winds two "dœgr," and land then lay before them, and upon it was a great wood and many wild beasts; an island lay off to the southeast, and there they found a bear, and they called this Biarney (Bear Island), while the land where the wood was they called Markland (Forest-land).

Biarni found the second land to which he came "flat and wooded," and the chronicler evidently intends to identify with it the second land he reports to have been discovered by Leif, which the latter named Markland. Leif, according to this writer, found it to be "a level wooded land, and there were broad stretches of white sand where they went, and the land was level by the sea." The narratives thus agree as to the woods, but the Saga does not add that the land was level. On the other hand it notes the offshore island to the southeast which they called Bear Island. Islands so named seem to have been very common, since, besides the two of this narrative, Graah tells us that the name was applied to Disko. It is evident that our chroniclers did not collaborate in their descriptions of Markland, since they agree in only one feature and that closely associated with the name by which that region came to be widely known.

The two versions of the Saga differ somewhat in their accounts of the next landfall. One says:

Thence they sailed southward along the land for a long time, and came to a cape; the land lay upon the starboard; there were long strands and sandy banks there. They rowed to the land and found upon the cape there the keel of a ship, and they called it there Kiarlarnes (Keelness); they also called the strands Furdustrandir (Wonder-strands), because they were so long to sail by.

The other runs as follows:

When two dœgr had elapsed, they descried land, and they sailed off this land; there was a cape to which they came. They beat into the wind along this coast, having the land on the starboard side. This was a bleak coast, with long and sandy shores. They went ashore in boats, and found the keel of a ship, so they called it Keelness there; they likewise gave a name to the strands and called them Wonder-strands, because they were so long to sail by.

The first version seems to regard Keelness and the Wonder-strands as attached to Markland, while the second implies that it was separated by another stretch of sea. There is no mention of these Wonder-strands in the Biarni narrative, but it is possible that the "broad stretches of white sand" connected with Markland in the Flat Island Book story of Leif's voyage may refer to them if the first version of the Saga quoted above is correct. There is no mention of Keelness here, but it is touched upon in this chronicler's account of the supposed earlier expedition of Thorvald. We shall mention this again but will insert here what concerns the naming of that cape. According to this narrative, then, the second summer Thorvald spent in Wineland he—

set out toward the east with the ship, and along the northern coast. They were met by a high wind off a certain promontary, and were driven ashore there, and damaged the keel of their ship, and were compelled to remain there for a long time and repair the injury to their vessel. Then said Thorvald to his companions: "I propose that we raise the keel upon this cape, and call it Keelness." And so they did.

To the eastward of this cape was a firth into which they afterward sailed, and there Thorvald met his death.

The Flat Island Book says that after leaving Markland, Leif and his companions sailed for 2 dœgr and came to an island on which was dew as sweet as honey. The "2 dœgr" and the crossing might be lined up with the firth to the east of Keelness in the second version of the Saga and so made to support it, just as the white sands of Markland may be quoted in support of the first, but nothing is said in this place of Keelness, and the island is more likely to reflect a memory of the Stream Isle to be mentioned presently. I am inclined to accept the first Saga version which is usually regarded as the more reliable, and the two may be reconciled by assuming that the landfalls were upon the same coast 2 dœgr apart.

The origin of the name Keelness raises an interesting question, and here again it seems to me that the account given in the Flat Island Book is the more probable. Evidently the keel is supposed to have belonged to a European vessel, and the likelihood of such an article drifting ashore from any European settlement is in the highest degree unlikely. The ocean current on the west side of Baffin Bay runs south, and if a keel drifted in from the Greenland settlements we must suppose it was carried northwest by that branch of the Gulf Stream which washes the west coast of Greenland and then south by the Labrador Current for over a thousand miles, and that all this took place between 985 or 986, when Greenland was settled, and the date of Karlsefni's voyage, about 1003—rapid work to have been accomplished within less than 20 years. It would seem that the same Labrador Current must have inhibited pretty effectively the appearance of a keel from Iceland, not settled until 874-930, or any region more remote. If the keel was left by an earlier Norse expedition, and the Saga is solely to be relied upon, it must have been that of Leif, in which case Karlsefni and his companions should have learned of it either then or later. This might be used as an argument that the voyage attributed to Thorvald actually took place, or that the naming of the cape belongs to a later time, that is, to Karlsefni's exploratory voyage to the north during which Thorvald was killed. The first supposition would, however, be open to the objection raised in the case of Leif. Unless, indeed, there is some truth in the account given in the Flat Island Book, I am disposed to believe that this cape was named for some other reason than that given in the Saga, perhaps from its appearance or from some natural feature nearby.

The Saga now continues as follows: "Then the country became indented with bays, and they steered their ships into a bay," and here is inserted the account of the two Gaels, Haki and Hækia, how on being sent southward to explore the country they brought back samples of self-sown wheat and grapes. It has been pointed out frequently that this is an interpolation, and it is clearly shown to be the case by the repetition contained in the last sentence, for it tells us that the Gaels were taken on board again "whereupon Karlsefni and his followers held on their way, until they came to where the coast was indented with bays. They stood into a bay with their ships."

To resume:

There was an island out at the mouth of the bay, about which there were strong currents, wherefore they called it Straumey (Stream Isle). There were so many birds there, that it was scarcely possible to step between the eggs. They sailed through the firth, and called it Straumfiord (Streamfirth), and carried their cargoes ashore from the ships, and established themselves there. They had brought with them all kinds of livestock. It was a fine country there. There were mountains thereabouts. They occupied themselves exclusively with the exploration of the country. They remained there during the winter, and they had taken no thought for this during the summer. The fishing began to fail, and they began to fall short of food. Then Thorhall the Huntsman disappeared. They had already prayed to God for food, but it did not come as promptly as their necessities seemed to demand. They searched for Thorhall for three half-days and found him on a projecting crag.

Being still a heathen, Thorhall is calling upon Thor for help, and a whale presently appears which they "capture." When they ate of it, however, they became sick and, learning of its supposed origin, they threw it into the sea, and again appealed to God, whereupon "the weather improved, and they could now row out to fish, and thenceforth they had no lack of provisions, for they could hunt game on the land, gather eggs on the island, and catch fish from the sea."

In the Flat Island Book the narrative covering this part of the route is very greatly condensed and is incorporated with the Wineland visit so closely that it is not at first easy to separate them. Nevertheless, it is evident that—treated as an expedition under command of Leif—it is covered in the following sentences:

They .... came to an island which lay to the northward off the land. There they went ashore and looked about them, the weather being fine, and they observed that there was dew upon the grass, and it so happened that they touched the dew with their hands, and touched their hands to their mouths, and it seemed to them that they had never before tasted anything so sweet as this. They went aboard their ship again and sailed into a certain sound, which lay between the island and a cape, which jutted out from the land on the north, and they stood in westering past the cape.

Instead of a story of supernatural food-charming we have one of honeydew grass, drawn presumably from the wonder stories of the period, but the geography corresponds. It does not correspond when transferred to Wineland to which the Flat Island Book immediately hitches it. Resuming the narrative as told in the Saga, we find that Thorhall decided to leave his companions at this time, and, taking nine men, all who would go with him, he sailed "northward beyond Wonder-strands," and past Keelness, but was driven to Ireland by westerly gales. There all were enslaved, and merchants reported that Thorhall lost his life.

This narrative presents us with two difficulties. We are told that Thorhall was going "in search of Wineland," and yet in a ditty he is said to have composed he expresses an intention to return home. Another difficulty is the identity of this Thorhall. He is called, not here but at a later point in the narrative, Thorhall the Huntsman. But there was another Thorhall, Gamli's son, an East-firth man, who had come from Iceland as co-commander with Biarni, Grimolf's son, on the vessel which accompanied that of Karlsefni. Nothing more is heard of him, though Biarni is mentioned several times and his fate by drowning at sea carefully recorded. Thorhall the Huntsman went to Streamfirth in the same ship as Eric's son Thorvald, Eric's daughter Freydis, and Thorvard, the latter's husband. Only three vessels are enumerated, but which of these was taken by Thorhall and which Thorhall took it? From what we know of the redoubtable character of Freydis it would seem unlikely that anyone would desert lightly with her vessel, and Biarni, in subsequent parts of the Saga, appears still in command of a vessel, the same in which he was ultimately lost. Again, on the face of it, it does not seem probable that a body of 160 men, more than 50 to the vessel, would have allowed one ship to be carried away to suit the whim of 10. Nor does it seem likely that a vessel capable of crossing the Atlantic was built at Streamfirth. I think we must either suppose there were more than three vessels or entertain doubt of this part of the narrative.

We now come to the last stage of the voyage, from Streamfirth to Wineland. The Saga, which distinguishes plainly between these two regions, says that after Thorhall's departure northward, Karlsefni—

cruised southward off the coast, with Snorri and Biarni, and their people. They sailed for a long time, and until they came at last to a river, which flowed down from the land into a lake, and so into the sea. There were great bars at the mouth of the river, so that it could only be entered at the height of the flood-tide. Karlsefni and his men sailed into the mouth of the river, and called it there Hop [a small land-locked bay]. They found self-sown wheat-fields on the land there, wherever there were hollows, and wherever there was hilly ground, there were vines. Every brook there was full of fish. They dug pits, on the shore where the tide rose highest, and when the tide fell, there were halibut in the pits. There were great numbers of wild animals of all kinds in the woods. They remained there half a month and enjoyed themselves, and kept no watch. They had their live stock with them.

In other words it was a kind of Garden of Eden to these inhabitants of the inhospitable north. The Saga continues:

Karlsefni and his followers had built their huts above the lake, some of their dwellings being near the lake, and others farther away. Now they remained there that winter. No snow came there, and all of their live-stock lived by grazing.

The Flat Island Book's description of Wineland is given in connection with Leif's supposed earlier voyage from Greenland:

At ebb-tide there were broad reaches of shallow water there, and they ran their ship aground there, and it was a long distance from the ship to the ocean; yet were they so anxious to go ashore that they could not wait until the tide should rise under their ship, but hastened to the land, where a certain river flows out from a lake. As soon as the tide rose beneath their ship, however, they took the boat and rowed to the ship, which they conveyed up the river, and so into the lake, where they cast anchor and carried their hammocks ashore from the ship, and built themselves booths there. They afterwards determined to establish themselves there for the winter, and they accordingly built a large house. There was no lack of salmon there either in the river or in the lake, and larger salmon than they had ever seen before. The country thereabouts seemed to be possessed of such good qualities that cattle would need no fodder there during the winters. There was no frost there in the winters, and the grass withered but little. The days and nights there were of more nearly equal length than in Greenland or Iceland. On the shortest day of winter the sun was up between "eyktarstad" and "dagmalastad."

Karlsefni, as we have already been informed, took with him "all kinds of cattle, as it was their intention to settle the country, if they could." Arrived safely at "Leif's booths," the Saga says they—

carried their hammocks ashore there. They were soon provided with an abundant and goodly supply of food, for a whale of good size and quality was driven ashore there, and they secured it, and flensed it, and had then no lack of provisions. The cattle were turned out upon the land, and the males soon became very restless and vicious; they had brought a bull with them. Karlsefni caused trees to be felled, and to be hewed into timbers, wherewith to load his ship, and the wood was placed upon a cliff to dry. They gathered somewhat of all of the valuable products of the land, grapes, and all kinds of game and fish, and other good things.

In the Saga we find a note which would indicate that there was a third tradition regarding Karlsefni's expedition to Wineland which would subtract something from its romantic character but would lend strength to the belief that such a voyage was made. "Some say," the chronicler notes parenthetically, "that Biarni and Freydis remained behind here [at Streamfirth] with a hundred men, and went no further; while Karlsefni and Snorri proceeded to the southward with forty men, tarrying at Hop barely two months, and returning again the same summer."

The two main narratives agree strikingly regarding the topography of the country visited, and the climate, except that the Flat Island Book goes a little farther than the Saga by stating that there was no "frost" there, as well as no snow. It specifies salmon as the kind of fish they found in both lake and river and does not mention "halibut," probably in reality flounders, which were caught along shore. The Saga makes no mention of the "large house" Leif is supposed to have erected, nor of the stockade which Karlsefni's men put about it later. Finally, the Saga says nothing of those quantities of grapes and vines, upon which the Flat Island Book lays so much stress in connection with every visit to Wineland. The whale we may guess to be a more appetizing replica of Thorhall's at Streamfirth.

One of our critics finds fault with Leif for supposedly leaving his vessel aground on the sands while he and his men land to examine the country, but must a voyager always specifiy that he has left such and such a man behind to look after his vessel when he sets foot ashore?

Surprisingly little is said in any of the narratives regarding explorations in Wineland. During Leif's visit as narrated in the Flat Island Book we are, indeed, told that the leader undertook this systematically, but the exploring parties were limited to points from which they could return by night, and the story is a build-up for the discovery of grapes by the German Tyrker. An important exception is in the account of Thorvald's assumed Wineland visit. According to this narrative he and his companions reached Wineland in the summer and—

remained there quietly during the winter, supplying themselves with food by fishing. In the spring, however, Thorvald said that they should put their ship in order, and that a few men should take the after-boat, and proceed along the western coast, and explore [that region] thereabouts during the summer. They found it a fair, well-wooded country; it was but a short distance from the woods to the sea, and [there were] white sands, as well as great numbers of islands and shallows. They found neither dwelling of man nor lair of beast; but in one of the westerly islands, they found a wooden building for the shelter of grain. They found no other trace of human handiwork, and they turned back, and arrived at Leif's-booths in the autumn.

The existence of a storehouse does not prove that there was a farming population in this country, since such buildings were used by the Indians for other purposes than the housing of cultivated cereals.

Since the Saga speaks only of explorations about Streamfirth, it has been thought by some that if there is any truth in the above narrative, it concerns explorations in that region, but the topography does not correspond. It rather suggests the southeastern coast of Massachusetts or some similar region. It is incredible that they expended no effort to extend their knowledge of the most delightful region they came in contact with.

The Wineland narratives concern themselves principally, however, with the inhabitants of that country, the people they call Skrellings. Here the two accounts show remarkable agreements and striking differences. According to each there were three encounters with these people, but the Saga states that the latter came by sea in skin canoes and the Flat Island Book that they arrived by land, out of the woods. On their first appearance, according to the Saga, the Skrellings did not land, but merely gazed at these new beings and then went away, on their second visit they were frightened away and turned hostile on account of the bellowing of a bull, and on their third appearance there was a fight. According to the Flat Island Book the Skrellings were frightened by the bull on their very first appearance and rushed to Karlsefni's house for shelter. He would not allow them to come in and presently they overcame their terror and laid down bundles of furs which they were carrying, whereupon a lively trade sprang up. They came back a second time to trade but fled because one of the Norsemen killed a Skrelling attempting to deprive him of his weapon. The third time they came to fight.

According to both narratives the Skrellings traded with furs, but according to the Saga the Norsemen purchased them with red cloth, while the Flat Island Book maintains it was with the milk of their cows. The Saga says nothing of the stockade which Karlsefni put up around his house after the first visit. Both agree that the Skrellings wanted to buy weapons but that Karlsefni and Snorri forbade the sale. According to the Saga the Norsemen were at first put to flight but were saved by an act of heroism on the part of Freydis, although only two Norsemen were killed while many enemies died. The Flat Island Book, however, indicates that Karlsefni arranged what must have been an ambuscade, 10 men showing themselves on a point of land near the sea while the remainder, fortified behind the redoubtable bull, concealed themselves in the forest. It seems that the attackers approached by land along the shore of the lake, between that and the forest, and were caught in flank by the Norsemen concealed in the woods and many of them were slain. This narrative implies, however, that they were ultimately frightened away by observing the effects of a Norse ax which the Skrelling chief, or one of the Skrelling chiefs, tested upon a companion with fatal effects. This episode, in somewhat different form, appears in the Saga. In that tale, however, the Skrelling wielding the ax is not said to have been a chief. He and his companions tried it out on a tree with satisfactory results, but when they attempted to use it on a stone it broke and they threw it away as of no value. In either form of this tale we have simply a Norse joke such as Indians often tell regarding the reactions of their own ancestors on first attempting to use European implements. But the Indians had axes and knew what to do with them, and they knew enough not to try them on stones or human beings, unless the human beings happened to be enemies or slaves.

During this encounter, as related by the Saga, the Skrellings resorted to a peculiar weapon the nature of which has caused much fruitless discussion. "The Skrellings raised up on a pole a great ballshaped body, almost the size of a sheep's belly, and nearly black in color, and this they hurled from the pole up on the land above Karlsefni's followers, and it made a frightful noise, where it fell." It was the fear which this aroused in the Norse which made them flee, so it would seem that the flight of both parties was based on superstitious dread. This aboriginal bomb finds representation in the Flat Island Book only in "a great crash" heard by those inside of the palisade during the second visit of the Skrellings. The Flat Island Book gives no intimation of the kinds of weapons used by these

Skrellings other than this, but the Saga says that they had "war-slings" and the skull of one Norseman, Thorbriand, Snorri's son, was cleft by a flat stone, presumably projected from one of these. And naturally, as the Skrellings are supposed to have advanced by land, nothing is said in the Flat Island Book of the "flails" of which the Saga speaks. It is interesting to note that one can make out the nature of the terrain on this first intercontinental battleground by close reading of the narratives. After the Norse had been frightened in the manner just indicated, the Saga goes on to say that "they could think of nought but flight, and of making their escape up along the river bank, for it seemed to them, that the troop of the Skrellings was rushing towards them from every side, and they did not pause until they came to certain jutting crags, where they offered a stout resistance," and after the victory they "returned to their dwellings, and bound up their wounds, and weighed carefully what throng of men that could have been, which had seemed to descend upon them from the land; it now seemed to them, that it could have been but the one party, that which came from the boats, and that the other troop must have been an ocular delusion." Now, the Flat Island Book says: "The lie of the land was such that the proposed meeting-place had the lake upon the one side, and the forest upon the other." The two narratives might be reconciled by supposing that the Skrellings had actually landed part of their company at some point from which they could come upon the Norsemen from the rear through the woods, while on leaving they all took to their boats. The nature of the country where the contest occurred seems evident, but there is some doubt as to which party ambushed which.

If we compare these two narratives on the ground of their relative plausibility, we find the balance inclines rather to the much-condemned Flat Island Book, aside from the cargoes of grapes with which the author of that narrative seems to have been obsessed. First, we do not know of skin canoes this far south. They belong to more northern regions. The weapons used also belong rather to the north, and the employment of flails swung in the air to declare war-like or peaceful intentions is otherwise unknown. These "flails" may have been spear throwers which are related to slings though never used so far as we know for hurling stones. They could hardly have been double paddles, for they are used with kayaks, and the skin canoes of these Skrellings do not seem to have been of that nature. Moreover, to continue our criticism, in making their attack, American aborigines would not ordinarily paddle in directly in front of the dwellings of their enemies. They would have come ashore some distance off and launched an attack from the land side in the early morning. As to the time of day we cannot say anything, but otherwise the Flat Island Book indicates the more probable maneuver unless on this point the Saga is to be interpreted as suggested above.

In the Flat Island Book there is mention of a supernatural visitant who appeared to Gudrid just at the outbreak of hostilities. Apparitions of this kind have been mentioned by both narratives in describing the events of the winter which Gudrid spent at Lysufirth, and it may possibly be explained by reference to these. The Saga tells us, it will be remembered, that Sigrid, the wife of Thorstein the Swarthy, sees the spirits of those of the company who had died that winter and among them her own although she was then living. It is possible, therefore, that the apparition which Gurid sees in Wineland and which calls itself Gudrid, although possessing some of the physical characteristics of the Skrellings in whose country this happened, was Gudrid's own ghost which came to indicate that her life was threatened, and its sudden disappearance a sign that events had postponed the sentence.

The nature of the Skrelling "bomb" has defied all attempts at explanation, though Schoolcraft thought he had discovered a clew in a former Chippewa custom. He learned that in their canoe fights these Indians sometimes used a big rock incased in skin which they elevated upon a pole and cast into an enemy's canoe in order to upset it. But there would be no point in hurling such an object upon the land, nor is there an adequate explanation of the loud noise which it made, impliedly due to bursting.

The use of milk by the Norsemen in trade has been ridiculed, but both narratives state that they had cattle with them, and milk would undoubtedly appeal to the aboriginal palate. The amount thus used in barter may very well have been exaggerated, the interest of the story turning, as in the case of the metal ax, on Skrelling reaction to a European novelty. On the face of it, trade in red cloth as described by the Saga is more probable, knowing as we do the fondness of our Indians for red fabrics, but one would like to inquire how Karlsefni learned in advance to provide himself with the amount of red cloth that is indicated. He was, indeed, a trader, but he had never had dealings with either Eskimo or Indians, and there is no evidence that he and his companions contemplated trade when they left Greenland. They are supposed to have anticipated settling in a country believed to be uninhabited. Traces of former occupants were found in Greenland when it was first settled but living Eskimo were not encountered until about 200 years later, and the other inhabitants of America were first revealed by this expedition.

Rupture of relations between the colonists and natives as the result of the slaughter of a Skrelling is more likely than that the bellowing of a bull should have caused it, though one writer has suggested that bovine animosity to the color red might have brought it about, since the Skrellings used the cloth they purchased largely to tie around their heads. On the other hand, since chroniclers normally prefer to record victories rather than defeats, the initial rout of the Norse in the final battle may perhaps indicate that the account of it in the Saga is more accurate, except for the direction from which the enemy approached.

The time of year when these events took place seems to be given more correctly in the Saga, judging by what we know of Indian customs. It places the first appearance of the Skrellings in the latter part of the summer in which the Norse came to Wineland or in the fall succeeding. They reappeared "when spring opened," and the attack was 3 weeks later. The Flat Island Book agrees that the aborigines put in their first appearance in summer, but this was "the summer succeeding the first winter" the white men spent in that country. Their second visit was made, however, shortly afterward "in the early part of the second winter," and the fight took place only a little later. If the third tradition is correct and Karlsefni and Snorri were in Wineland only 2 months, all this has to be enormously compressed. Finally it should be said that the differences in these narratives are the strongest points in their favor. They are factual but show no evidence of copying.

The Saga continues:

It now seemed clear to Karlsefni and his people that, although the country thereabouts was attractive, their life would be one of constant dread and turmoil by reason of the [hostility of the] inhabitants of the country, so they forthwith prepared to leave, and determined to return to their own country. They sailed to the northward off the coast, and found five Skrellings, clad in skin-doublets, lying asleep near the sea. There were vessels beside them, containing animal marrow, mixed with blood. Karlsefni and his company concluded that they must have been banished from their own land. They put them to death.

Students do not seem to have discovered that a duplicate but much distorted account of this adventure has been inserted farther on in the Saga. It reads as follows:

When they sailed away from Wineland, they had a southerly wind, and so came upon Markland, where they found five Skrellings, of whom one was bearded, two were women, and two were children. Karlsefni and his people took the boys, but the others escaped, and these Skrellings sank down into the earth. They bore the lads away with them, and taught them to speak, and they were baptized. They said, that their mother's name was Vætilldi, and their father's Uvægi. They said, that kings governed the Skrellings, one of whom was called Avalldamon, and the other Valldidida. They stated, that there were no houses there, and that the people lived in caves or holes. They said, that there was a land on the other side over against their country, which was inhabited by people who wore white garments, and yelled loudly, and carried poles before them, to which rags were attached; and people believed that this must have been Hvitramannaland (White-men's-land), or Ireland the Great.[2]

Except for the finding of five Skrellings, this differs so much from the encounter just mentioned that it is not surprising that its real character has failed of detection. All the more as the event is placed in Markland, between Streamfirth and Greenland, and it has been assumed that Streamfirth was part of Wineland. But except in this one place the Saga never makes this last assumption. When Karlsefni was at Streamfirth, Thorhall is said to have left "in search of Wineland," and Karlsefni went south shortly afterward in quest of the same region. Although the Flat Island Book confuses the two to some extent, it is the southern region, where "Leif's booths" were erected, that is constantly called Wineland. The name is never used for a region farther north. The name "Markland" may have been employed in this episode because the event occurred in a wooded country—Markland may have been a general term covering Streamfirth and the territories north and south of it, or—and I believe this is the principal explanation—there has also been some confusion between this event and Karlsefni's later expedition in search of Thorhall during which Thorvald was killed.

It is to be noted that, if this episode and that regarding the two Gaels are removed from the Saga, little of the miraculous is left except for the events at Lysufirth in Greenland, and the adventure with the Uniped which itself is under some suspicion. We shall take that up below. The names reported as given by the Skrelling children look more like myth names than names of Indian or Eskimo extraction though the latter explanation is possible.

Reverting to the Saga, we find it noted next that, having killed the five Skrellings, Karlsefni's people "afterwards found a cape,

---

[2] "Or Ireland the Great" is omitted in one manuscript. For a careful discussion of Hvitramannaland or Ireland the Great see L. D. Scisco, "The Tradition of Hvitramannaland," in the American Historical Magazine, vol. 3, pp. 379-388 and 515-524, 1908. He concludes rather plausibly that the region originally intended was western Ireland.

upon which there was a great number of animals, and this cape looked as if it were one cake of dung, by reason of the animals which lay there at night." It is more likely that this was a bird rookery, the appearance of which is often described in these terms. Thus Stearns (1884, pp. 250-251) says of Shag Rocks on the southern coast of Labrador near St. Mary Islands where cormorants (or shags) bred in numbers:

> At a distance these rocks present the appearance of being covered with snow, but a nearer approach shows that this is a covering of guano from the continual droppings of the birds; while the tops of the rocks are thickly embedded with an accumulation of guano from the same cause, firmly stamped down with the continual pattering of numberless feet.

"They now arrived again at Streamfirth, where they found great abundance of all those things of which they stood in need." Again the Streamfirth episode and all that happened between the departure of the colonists from Wineland and their arrival in Greenland is omitted by the Flat Island Book with the exception of one or two occurrences which appear, not in this connection, but in describing a supposed earlier expedition of Thorvald.

This introduces us to one of the most perplexing chapters in the Wineland sagas, the circumstances surrounding the death of this brother of Leif. The Saga of Eric the Red gives the story as follows:

> Karlsefni then set out [from Steamfirth] with one ship, in search of Thorhall the Huntsman, but the greater part of the company remained behind. They sailed to the northward around Keelness, and then bore to the westward, having land to the larboard. The country there was a wooded wilderness, as far as they could see, with scarcely an open space; and when they had journeyed a considerable distance, a river flowed down from the east toward the west. They sailed into the mouth of the river, and lay to by the southern bank.
>
> It happened one morning that Karlsefni and his companions discovered in an open space in the woods above them, a speck, which seemed to shine toward them, and they shouted at it; it stirred, and it was a Uniped, who skipped down to the bank of the river by which they were lying. Thorvald, a son of Eric the Red, was sitting at the helm, and the Uniped shot an arrow into his inwards. Thorvald drew out the arrow, and exclaimed: "There is fat around my paunch; we have hit upon a fruitful country, and yet we are not like to get much profit of it." Thorvald died soon after from this wound. Then the Uniped ran away back toward the north, Karlsefni and his men pursued him, and saw him from time to time. The last they saw of him, he ran down into a creek. Then they turned back; whereupon one of the men recited this ditty:

> Eager, our men, up hill down dell,
>   Hunted a Uniped;
> Hearken, Karlsefni, while they tell
>   How swift the quarry fled!

Then they sailed away back toward the north, and believed they had got sight of the land of the Unipeds; nor were they disposed to risk the lives of their men longer. They concluded that the mountains of Hop, and those which they had now found, formed one chain, and this appeared to be so because they were about an equal distance removed from Streamfirth, in either direction.

As already observed, the Flat Island Book version of this is inserted in an account of a supposed visit of Thorvald to Wineland. According to this narrative, the second summer they spent there they set out on an exploring expedition toward the north in course of which they came upon and named Keelness as already described. The narrative then continues as follows:

Then they sailed away to the eastward off the land, and into the mouth of the adjoining firth, and to a headland, which projected into the sea there, and which was entirely covered with woods. They found an anchorage for their ship, and put out the gangplank to the land, and Thorvald and all of his companions went ashore. "It is a fair region here," said he, "and here I should like to make my home." They then returned to the ship, and discovered on the sands, in beyond the headland, three skin-canoes, with three men under each. They thereupon divided their party, and succeeded in seizing all of the men but one, who escaped with his canoe. They killed the eight men, and then ascended the headland again, and looked about them, and discovered within the firth certain hillocks, which they concluded must be habitations. They were then so overpowered with sleep that they could not keep awake, and all fell into a [heavy] slumber, from which they were awakened by the sound of a cry uttered above them; and the words of the cry were these: "Awake, Thorvald, thou and all thy company, if thou wouldst save thy life; and board thy ship with all thy men, and sail with all speed from the land!" A countless number of skin-canoes then advanced toward them from the inner part of the firth, thereupon Thorvald exclaimed: "We must put out the warboards on both sides of the ship, and defend ourselves to the best of our ability, but offer little attack." This they did, and the Skrellings, after they had shot at them for a time, fled precipitately, each as best he could. Thorvald then inquired of his men, whether any of them had been wounded, and they informed him that no one of them had received a wound. "I have been wounded in my arm-pit," says he; "an arrow flew in between the gunwale and the shield, below my arm. Here is the shaft, and it will bring me to my end! But me ye shall convey to that headland which seemed to me to offer so pleasant a dwelling-place; thus it may be fulfilled, that the truth sprang to my lips, when I expressed the wish to abide there for a time. Ye shall bury me there, and place a cross at my head, and another at my feet, and call it Crossness for ever after." At that time Christianity had obtained in Greenland; Eric the Red died, however, before [the introduction of] Christianity. Thorvald died, and when they had carried out his instructions, they took their departure, and rejoined their companions [in Wineland], and they told each other of the experiences which had befallen them.

Thorvald's companions remained in Wineland during the following winter, and then went back to Greenland with the usual load of grapes and wood.

As these two narratives stand, apart from the beginning and end, the second is the more probable, Unipeds not having yet attained scientific status, and there being considerable mystery about the entrance and exit of this particular specimen. All the details in the Flat Island Book story are credible except the warning voice, and this might have been etherealized by the chronicler or might actually have been heard in a dream by Thorvald. Although the sleep from which the explorers were so rudely awakened is apparently supposed to have been supernaturally induced, we may read into it an early morning attack in accordance with Indian custom. Here, instead of in Wineland, the Flat Island Book introduces skin canoes. It has been assumed that the chronicler has transferred these from the Wineland experiences, but, except for the superior reputation acquired by the Saga, the reverse is the more probable, since skin canoes are known historically in the north instead of the south. If the "flails" of the Winelanders were spear throwers and they had slings, while the Marklanders fought with bows and arrows, the condition was exactly the reverse of what we should expect, spear throwers having been known in historic times among the Eskimo but not in New England. To be sure we do not know positively that the Markland arrows were projected by bows, but this seems to have been assumed by the chroniclers. The use of arrows here, be it noted, is affirmed by both documents. Both the Uniped and the Skrellings use them.

Mention was made above of the probable confusion between two different stories of an encounter with five Skrellings and the possible confusion of these with the story of the nine Skrellings met by Thorvald according to the Flat Island Book narrative. While these differ widely in details, there are suspicious cross-resemblances. In two of them five Skrellings are mentioned. In one the Skrellings are asleep, and the same may be assumed of the nine Skrellings who were found under their canoes. In all cases the Norsemen attack them, killing all in one case, and all but one in another, and capturing two in a third. While one of these encounters is said to have taken place between Wineland and Streamfirth, another is placed in Markland and the third in or near Markland.

After Karlsefni returned from the land of the Unipeds, he and his company—

passed the winter at Streamfirth. Then the men began to divide into factions, of which the women were the cause; and those who were without wives endeavored to seize upon the wives of those who were married, whence trouble arose. Snorri, Karlsefni's son, was born the first autumn, and he was three winters old [when they left].

After this comes the second story of the five Skrellings which, as I have already said, I believe to be a later insertion, and the Saga concludes the account of this voyage by saying, "Now they arrived in Greenland, and remained during the winter with Eric the Red." From the above it would appear that Snorri was born in the autumn of 1003 and it was in 1006 when they returned to Greenland. The Flat Island Book tells us that Snorri was born during the second summer his parents passed in Wineland which, following that document, would be in 1009, and the return to Greenland in 1010.

The Flat Island Book brings Karlsefni and his party directly to Greenland from Wineland the summer after their battle with the Skrellings. The Saga has nothing more to say regarding Wineland voyages. The rest of it is taken up with the fate of Biarni, Grimolf's son, who lost his life at sea in the foundering of his vessel, and an account of Karlsefni's return to Iceland with Gudrid and an enumeration of his descendants.

The fate of Grimolf's son has no particular bearing on our attempts to locate the several landfalls of the Norsemen in America except as it tends strongly to support the credibility of the Saga of Eric the Red in which it is related, for it tells us that his ship foundered because they "came into a sea, which was filled with worms." These "worms" were of course the teredo, and those who are now concerned with proofing timber against them will be interested in reading: "They had a boat, which had been coated with seal-tar; this the sea-worm does not penetrate."

The Flat Island Book, however, tells of another expedition to Wineland, one which had a tragic ending. According to this, during the summer in which Karlsefni returned from that country, a vessel came to Greenland from Norway commanded by two brothers named Helgi and Finnbogi. Freydis, Eric's daughter, induced them to undertake a voyage to Wineland the summer following. Both vessels arrived safely but during the winter Freydis compassed the death of the brothers and all their companions, male and female, and returned to Greenland the summer after that in their ship, laden with the products of the country. Freydis attempted to frighten those with her into silence regarding what had taken place, but Leif finally discovered it. He had no heart to punish her, it is said, perhaps on account of the service she had rendered Karlsefni and his men during the battle with the Skrellings, but it is added regarding her and her weak-minded husband—the two seem to have been counterparts of Lord and Lady Macbeth—that "no one from that time forward thought them worthy of aught but evil." This supposed voyage has elicited much hostile criticism, and we would fain wish that it might have been a work of the imagination, but unfortunately feminine human nature has shown itself to as ill advantage on more than one historic occasion, and a tragedy of this kind might help to account for the termination of visits to Wineland. Between the Skrellings and this horrible event they may have become associated with ill luck.

As in the case of the Saga, the last paragraphs of this narrative are taken up with the return of Karlsefni to Iceland and the story of his descendants. It differs, however, in inserting a visit to Norway where "he sold his wares, and both he and his wife were received with great favor by the most distinguished men of Norway." They then prepared to return to Iceland, but here an item of interest to us is introduced.

When all his preparations had been made, and his ship lying at the wharf, awaiting favorable winds, there came to him a Southerner, a native of Bremen in the Saxonland, who wished to buy his "house-neat" (a weather-vane, or other ornament at the point of the gable of a house or upon a ship). "I do not wish to sell it." said he. "I will give thee half a 'mörk' in gold for it," says the Southerner. This Karlsefni thought a good offer, and accordingly closed the bargain. The Southerner went his way, with the house-neat, and Karlsefni knew not what wood it was, but it was mösur, come from Wineland.

This is the "mausur" wood of which the Saga speaks. The latter begins its account of Wineland with a reference to this mysteriously valuable wood, generally regarded as maple, and perhaps bird's-eye maple, while the Flat Island Book here ends with an equally dramatic reference to it.

SUMMARY OF THE EXPEDITIONS

Before going farther I shall attempt an outline of the probable course of events of which these Wineland sagas profess to treat.

The Saga of Eric the Red is undoubtedly the more trustworthy of the two narratives, but this trustworthiness applies particularly to its treatment of the voyage of Karlsefni, and we may suspect that the story of Wineland was a much longer one and that many details have been suppressed. The relation of Leif's supposed discovery of Wineland would give the impression that he reached it after crossing the full breadth of the North Atlantic without coming in sight of any intervening lands, but we must suppose that he kept far enough to the north to be in the neighborhood of Iceland and the east coast of Greenland though apparently without sighting either. While such a voyage was possible it is highly improbable, and I am inclined to accept the story substantially as related in the Flat Island Book. All this requires us to believe is that a navigator called Biarni sailing west with the wind and ocean current in his favor was caught off the southern end of Greenland by a north wind and carried within sight of the Newfoundland coast and that, after sighting land in two more places, he finally reached Greenland. It is not necessary to accept all the details, but it is reasonable to suppose that Leif heard of this voyage and the new lands to the west and undertook to visit them himself, that he continued on farther south than Biarni to Nova Scotia or the New England coast, and that the Saga of Eric the Red has implanted a brief statement of the results of his expedition into the account of his return from Norway to Greenland, the one expedition having followed closely upon the other.

Leif's propagandizing work in Greenland was probably before this voyage. Whether he rescued the mariners at sea before or after it is of secondary importance, but there would have been an additional reason for calling him Leif the Lucky if he could report the discovery of a land of wood and grapes. Whether Biarni's voyage is or is not apochryphal, Leif was evidently the discoverer of Wineland, and to that discovery belong the two myths of the finding of grapes. As to the other events of Leif's voyage as told in the Flat Island Book, they are apparently mixed up with those reported for the voyage of Thorfinn Karlsefni except for the two first landfalls. It is quite certain that every Greenland navigator who visited Wineland carried back wood with him, and we are told in the Saga that Leif also took samples of self-sown wheat and vines.

The Flat Island Book has evidently mixed up the story of Thorbiorn's voyage to Greenland and subsequent settlement near Eric with that of the shipwrecked mariners. Neither story of the naming of Keelness is satisfactory. On one hand the drifting ashore of the keel from a European vessel on this part of the American coast is in the highest degree unlikely, and on the other, if the cape had been named by an earlier Norse expedition, Karlsefni should have known of the circumstances.

Since there is no mention of the voyage of Thorvald in the Saga, and since some of the events attributed to it are given by the latter as having happened during the expedition of Karlsefni, I omit it and place next the abortive venture of Thorstein, but am not sure whether the episode involving Eric's part in the expedition belongs here or with the earlier voyage of Leif. Here I am inclined, however, to follow the Flat Island Book and assume it was the latter, particularly as this authority tells us that Eric changed his intention to accompany the explorers and returned home. The Saga wishes us to believe that when Eric was thrown from his horse, some of his ribs were broken and his shoulder dislocated but that he was not deterred thereby from venturing out upon the tempestuous seas with Thorstein, and that the whole company, including apparently Eric, were "in high spirits." Leif might well have wished his fortunate father along, but the fact that Leif himself reaped the reputation for the discovery shows that Eric was not with him. We may follow the Saga in assuming that Thorstein did not marry Gudrid until after his return, and accept its version of their reason for going to Lysufirth to live, and the events which took place there, aside from the supernatural accompaniments. We should probably follow it in the main in its relation of the Karlsefni voyage, but should leave out the story of the two Gaelic runners and set down the second story of the five Skrellings as a later amplification of the first. I accept the narrative of Karlsefni's voyage to the north in search of Thorhall but would substitute the manner of Thorvald's death as related in the Flat Island Book for the adventure with the Uniped. However, there seems to be some confusion between the adventure with the nine Skrellings found under skin canoes and the two encounters in which five Skrellings figure. It is likely that real skin canoes were seen here for the first time, if at all, whereas those seen in Wineland were really of bark, or perhaps the Flat Island Book is correct in stating that the Wineland Skrellings always came through the woods. At least there seems to be evidence that their final attack was made by land, a maneuver which would be more in keeping with Indian strategy than a frontal assault. The aboriginal bomb may introduce a supernatural element impossible of explanation. The narratives agree that the main battle took place between the lake shore and a forest. If these Skrellings were armed with slings or spear throwers and those encountered farther north with bows and arrows, we have a curious violation of our expectations. Has the Saga inverted the facts and the Winelanders had bows and arrows while the northern Indians or Eskimo were provided with slings and spear throwers? Or did the southern Indians retain the use of slings and spear throwers after the northern Indians or Eskimo had adopted bows and arrows? A tantalizing insight is suggested into the history of weapons in America but it must remain such.

The exploration of the coast westward from Hop, as described in the account of Thorvald's voyage in the Flat Island Book, belongs probably to the voyage of Karlsefni and to a period before the Skrellings appeared, though it may have happened during Leif's expedition. Whether the encounter with the five Skrellings actually occurred, as the Saga indicates, during the return voyage from Wineland to Streamfirth, or was an event in the search northward of Streamfirth for Thorhall we cannot say, but I incline to the latter view. The cape covered with excrement was no doubt the breeding place of sea birds instead of the resort of animals. The principal event during the stay of Karlsefni's party at Streamfirth on their return to that place was the expedition in search of Thorhall and the death of Thorvald, which has already been alluded to.

I am not inclined to reject entirely the story of Freydis' expedition to Wineland, gruesome as it is. It is very likely that the tragedy which took place at that time may have converted the thought of Wineland the Good into the thought of Wineland the Unlucky, and may have added another inhibition to the fear of Skrellings and so prevented further exploitation of the country. It would, indeed, be surprising if only two voyages were made to Wineland. At least we know that Greenlanders sometimes ventured as far as Markland, for in the year 1347 a small Greenland vessel entered an Iceland fiord driven by storms after having visited Markland, and it is unlikely that it was the only one to attempt to bring wood from that country in later times.

CHRONOLOGY ACCORDING TO THE SAGA OF ERIC THE RED

999. Leif goes to visit Olaf Tryggvason in Norway.

999-1000. Winter spent in Norway.

1000. Leif returns to Greenland, visiting Wineland on the way.

1000-1001. Winter spent in Greenland.

1001. Thorstein Ericsson's fruitless expedition.

1001-1002. Winter spent in Greenland and at Lysufirth.

1002. Thorfinn Karlsefni comes to Greenland.

1002-1003. Winter spent in Greenland.

1003. Thorfinn Karlsefni reaches Streamfirth.

1003-1004. Winter spent at Streamfirth.

1004. Thorfinn Karlsefni reaches Wineland; Thorhall goes to Ireland.

1004-1005. Winter spent in Wineland.

1005. Thorfinn Karlsefni reaches Streamfirth on his return.

1005-1006. Winter spent at Streamfirth.

1006. Thorfinn Karlsefni returns to Greenland.

Possibly the dates after 1001 are too short by one year.

CHRONOLOGY ACCORDING TO THE FLAT ISLAND BOOK

985 or 986. Biarni's voyage from Iceland to Greenland via America.
        999. Leif in Norway.
1000-1001. Biarni in Norway.
     1001. Biarni returns to Greenland and Leif goes to Wineland.
1001-1002. Leif in Wineland.
     1002. Leif returns to Greenland.
1002-1003. Leif in Greenland.
     1003. Thorvald goes to Wineland.
1003-1004. Thorvald in Wineland.
     1004. Thorvald explores coast to westward.
1004-1005. Thorvald in Wineland.
     1005. Thorvald explores toward the north and is killed.
1005-1006. Thorvald's companions remain in Wineland.
     1006. Thorvald's companions return to Greenland.
     1006. Thorstein's fruitless voyage.
1006-1007. Thorstein and Gudrid at Lysufirth; Thorstein dies.
     1007. Thorfinn Karlsefni comes to Greenland.
1007-1008. Thorfinn Karlsefni at Brattahlid in Greenland.
     1008. Thorfinn Karlsefni reached Wineland.
1008-1009. Thorfinn Karlsefni in Wineland.
     1009. Thorfinn in Wineland; war with Skrellings.
1009-1010. Thorfinn in Wineland.
     1010. Thorfinn returns to Greenland.
1010-1011. All remain in Greenland.
     1011. Freydis goes to Wineland with Helgi and Finnbogi.
1011-1012. In Wineland; Freydis kills Helgi and Finnbogi and companions.
     1012. Freydis returns to Greenland; Thorfinn goes to Norway.
1012-1013. Thorfinn and Gudrid in Norway.
     1013. Thorfinn and Gudrid go to Iceland.

AN ATTEMPT TO IDENTIFY THE REGIONS VISITED

When one considers the limited data one has to depend upon in attempting to locate the points visited by the heroes of these narratives and the plausible variations in interpretation of key portions of the original texts, the multiplicity of theories based upon them is easily explained, and the skepticism of certain writers readily understood. Nevertheless, a conservative discussion of probabilities will, I believe, yield some satisfactory results. At any rate I propose to attempt it. We shall have to depend almost entirely on the Saga of Eric the Red, and specifically on the story of Thorfinn Karlsefni contained in it, though the Flat Island Book will be found to yield evidence which is not to be ignored.

First I will introduce a table of items regarding the most important regions to be identified, wherein (S) signifies Saga of Eric the Red, and (F) the Flat Island Book.

DATA FOR THE IDENTIFICATION OF SITES MENTIONED IN THE WINELAND SAGAS

Note: A dœgr was 12-hours sailing time, but the distance covered in that time varied widely, being given as from 50 miles to 200.

HELLULAND:

2 dœgr from Bear Id. southward (S).

"Large flat stones, and many of these were twelve ells wide" (S).

"There were many Arctic foxes" (S).

3 dœgr from Markland; 4 from Greenland (F) (Biarni).

Reached from Markland with "southwesterly gales" (F).

"High and mountainous, with ice-mountains upon it" (F).

On turning away for Greenland they found this was an island (F).

On leaving they still had a southwest wind (F) (Biarni).

Leif found "no grass there" (F).

"Great ice mountains lay inland back from the sea, and it was a [table-land of] flat rock all the way from the sea to the ice mountains" (F).

To Biarni it seemed "entirely devoid of good qualities" (F).

MARKLAND:

Reached by sailing 2 dœgr from Helluland with northerly winds (S).

"Upon it was a great wood" (S).

"And many wild beasts" (S).

"An island lay off to the southeast, where they found a bear" and so named it Biarney (S).

According to one account 2 dœgr from next land; according to another apparently a coast continuous with it (S).

Reached by "a southerly wind" from Wineland (S).

2 dœgr from another land "level and covered with woods," and with "small hillocks upon it" (F) (Biarni).

Reached by a "fair," presumably south wind (F) (Biarni).

"A flat and wooded country" (F) (Biarni).

(Leif): "a level wooded land, and there were broad stretches of white sand, where they went, and the land was level by the sea" (F).

The land of the Unipeds seems to have been near or in it (S).

WONDER-STRANDS AND KEELNESS:

(Version 1): reached by sailing "southward for a long time." when they "came to a cape; the land lay upon the starboard; there were long strands and sandy banks there" (S).

Found keel of a ship upon the cape and called it Keelness (S).

Strands called Furdustrandir (Wonder-strands) "because they were so long to sail by" (S).

(Version 2): reached in 2 dœgr from Markland (S).

"They sailed off this land; there was a cape to which they came" (S).

"They beat into the wind along this coast, having the land upon the starboard side. This was a bleak coast, with long and sandy shores" (S).

(Naming of Keelness and Wonder-strands given same way) (S).

"Then the country became indented with bays" (S).

Gaels put ashore after passing Wonder-strands (S).

Thorhall sails from Streamfirth "past Wonder-strands and Keelness, intending to cruise to the westward around the cape" (S).

Karlsefni sails from Streamfirth in search of Thorhall "northward around Keelness, and then bears to the westward, having land to the larboard"; comes to a river flowing from east to west in wooded wilderness; sails "back to north" on leaving (S).

Thorvald's ship driven ashore by a high wind after he had set out from Wineland "toward the east" and "along the northern coast." The ship repaired there and keel set up upon cape, which is therefore called Keelness (F).

Sails "eastward off the land, and into the mouth of the adjoining firth, and to a headland covered entirely with woods" (F).

STREAMFIRTH (STRAUMFIORD), AND STRAUMEY (STREAM ISLE):

Coming to a country indented with bays they entered one at the mouth of which was an island "about which there were strong currents, wherefore they called it Straumey (Stream Isle). There were so many birds there, that it was scarcely possible to step between the eggs" (S).

"They sailed through the firth" (S).

Established themselves there for the winter with "all kinds of livestock" (S).

"It was a fine country" (S).

"There were mountains thereabouts" (S).

"They occupied themselves exclusively with the exploration of the country" (S).

In consequence when "fishing began to fail they began to fall short of food" (S).

Capture a whale but made ill from eating it (S).

Situation improves later and "they could hunt game on the land, gather eggs on the island, and catch fish from the sea" (S).

Though Gaels had found grapes according to an earlier part of episode, Thorhall's ditty indicates that they had not (S).

Karlsefni "sailed for a long time" from here to reach Wineland (S).

To reach it he "cruised southward off the coast," and on his return "sailed to the northward off the coast" (S).

Returned to Streamfirth in spring or early summer, "and found great abundance of all those things of which they stood in need" (S).

Mountains in "Land of the Unipeds" believed to form one chain with those of Hop "because they were about an equal distance removed from Streamfirth, in either direction" (S).

Perhaps referred to in the following passages in (F): After leaving Markland they "sailed away upon the main with north-east winds," and sighted land after 2 dœgr. "They sailed towards this land, and came to an island which lay to the northward off the land" (F).

Dew sweet to the taste found there (F).

"They went aboard their ship again and sailed into a certain sound, which lay between the island and a cape which jutted out from the

land on the north, and they stood in westering past the cape." (F).
(The above may, however, have been in Wineland.)

WINELAND:

Leif is reported to have reached Wineland directly from Norway finding "self-sown wheat fields and vines growing there. There were also those trees there which are called 'mausur,' and of all these they took specimens. Some of the timbers were so large that they were used in building" (S).

This was in the summer of 1000 (S).

(Gaels said to have found self-sown wheat and grapes by running south from Streamfirth) (S).

Karlsefni comes to it by cruising southward "off the coast" from Streamfirth (S).

"They sailed for a long time" (S).

There was "a river, which flowed down from the land into a lake, and so into the sea. There were great bars at the mouth of the river, so that it could only be entered at the height of the flood-tide," so they called it Hop (S).

"They found self-sown wheat fields on the land there, wherever there were hollows, and wherever there was hilly ground, there were vines" (S).

"Every brook there was full of fish. They dug pits, on the shore where the tide rose highest, and when the tide fell, there were halibut in the pits" (S).

"There were great numbers of animals of all kinds in the woods" (S).

"They had their live-stock with them" (S).

"Skrellings" come "in skin-canoes, and staves were brandished from the boats, with a noise like flails, and they were revolved in the same direction in which the sun moves; when they came to fight these were revolved in the opposite direction" (S).

"They were swarthy men, and ill-looking, and the hair of their heads was ugly. They had great eyes, and were broad of cheek" (S).

They came from the southward around a point (S).

"No snow came there [the first winter] and all of their live-stock lived by grazing" (S).

The Skrellings bought red cloths, exchanging for them "peltries and quite gray skins"; bound cloth about heads (S).

They also desired to buy "swords and spears," but it was forbidden (S).

Skrellings scared away owing to bellowing of a bull and come back to fight (S).

"The Skrellings had war-slings" (S).

They raised on a pole "a great ballshaped body, almost the size of a sheep's belly, and nearly black in color." They hurled it up on the land "and it made a frightful noise, where it fell" (S).

Norse fled up along river bank "until they came to certain jutting crags, where they offered a stout resistance" (S).

Forest near the lake (S).

One Norseman had "his skull cleft by a flat stone" (S).

Had "delusion" of being attacked by another party from the forest (S).

On leaving the country Karlsefni "sailed to the northward off the coast" (S).

Find five Skrellings "clad in skin-doublets," and with "vessels beside them, containing animal marrow, mixed with blood" (S).

Mountains of Hop and those of Uniped country equally distant (from Streamfirth) (S).

"When they sailed away from Wineland, they had a southerly wind, and so came upon Markland" (S).

(F) See above for possible items.

"At ebb-tide there were broad reaches of shallow water there, and they ran their ship aground there, and it was a long distance from the ship to the ocean; yet were they so anxious to go ashore that they could not wait until the tide should rise under their ship, but hastened to the land, where a certain river flows out from a lake. As soon as the tide rose beneath their ship, however, they took the boat and rowed to the ship, which they conveyed up the river, and so into the lake, where they cast anchor and carried their hammocks ashore from the ship, and built themselves booths there. They afterwards determined to establish themselves there for the winter, and they accordingly built a large house" (F).

"There was no lack of salmon there either in the river or in the lake, and larger salmon than they had ever seen before" (F).

"The country thereabouts seemed to be possessed of such good qualities that cattle would need no fodder there during the winters. There was no frost there in the winters, and the grass withered but little" (F).

"The days and nights there were of more nearly equal length than in Greenland or Iceland. On the shortest day of winter the sun was up between 'eyktarstad' and 'dagmalastad'" (F).

They explore country no farther than each party can return in a day and a German among them finds grapes (F).

Each day they gathered grapes or "cut vines" and felled trees with which to load their ship (F).

Thorvald and his party supplied themselves with food their first winter in Wineland by fishing (F).

Next summer "a few men" take "the after-boat, and proceed along the western coast, and explore [the region] thereabouts during the summer. They found it a fair, well-wooded country; it was but a short distance from the woods to the sea, and [there were] white sands, as well as great numbers of islands and shallows. They found neither dwelling of man nor lair of beast; but in one of the westerly islands, they found a wooden building for the shelter of grain. They found no other trace of human handiwork, and they turned back, and arrived at Leif's-booths in the autumn" (F).

Next summer "Thorvald set out toward the east with the ship and along the northern coast," and came to Keelness (F).

Thorvald's companions return to Wineland, spend winter and take load of grapes and wood back to Greenland (F).

Karlsefni on going to Wineland took "all kinds of cattle, as it was their intention to settle the country, if they could" (F).

A whale of good size furnishes them with food (F).

"The cattle were turned out upon the land and the males soon became very restless and vicious; they had brought a bull with them" (F).

Wood was hewed into timbers and "placed upon a cliff to dry" (F).

"They gathered somewhat of all of the valuable products of the land, grapes, and all kinds of game and fish, and other good things" (F).

Skrellings come from woods, are frightened by a bull, and come with their packs to the house. They trade "gray furs, sables, and all kinds of peltries" for milk. They want to obtain weapons but this is forbidden (F).

Karlsefni has a palisade constructed about the house (F).

Karlsefni arranges a battle between the forest and the lake (F).

Return to Greenland with "vines, and grapes and peltries" (F).

A similar load brought back next year by Freydis (F).

Although written in a skeptical spirit, the treatment by J. P. McLean (1892, pp. 38-39) of early attempts to locate points in the Western World touched by the Norse makes a good introduction to this subject:

Torfæus who awakened interest in the subject in 1705, was content to place the scene in America, without even attempting to name the localities. In 1755, Paul Henri Mallet, in his "Histoire de Dannemarc", locates the scene in Labrador and Newfoundland. Robertson, in 1778, in his "History of America", although with misgivings, thinks "that the situation of Newfoundland corresponds best with that of the country discovered by the Norwegians." M. C. Sprengel (1782), in his "Geschichte der Entdeck Ungen", thinks they went as far south as Carolina. In 1793, Muñoz, in his "Historia del Nuevo Mundo", puts Vinland in Greenland. Barrow, in his "Voyages to the Arctic Regions" (1818), places Vinland in Labrador or Newfoundland. Hugh Murray, in his "Discoveries and Travels in North America" (1829), doubts the assigning of Vinland to America. Henry Wheaton (1831), in his "History of the Northmen", thought Vinland should be looked for in New England. Bancroft, the most eminent of American Historians, in the original third edition (1840) of his history, says "Scandinavians may have reached the shores of Labrador; the soil of the United States has not one vestige of their presence." Wilson (1862), in his "Prehistoric Man," declares that "Markland, . . . so far as the name or description can guide us, might be anywhere on the American coast," and that Nantucket is referred to is assumed, because they spoke of the dew upon the grass, because it tasted sweet. Foster, in his "Prehistoric Races of the United States" (1873), abruptly dismisses the subject, speaking of it as conjecture and no memorials having been left behind. Nadaillic (1883) speaks of the Norse discovery as "legends in which a little truth is mixed with much fiction." Weise, in his "Discoveries of America" (1884), believes the sea-rovers did not even pass Davis' Straits.

Attempts at identification by later writers are as follows:

IDENTIFICATION BY VARIOUS WRITERS OF REGIONS MENTIONED IN THE WINELAND NARRATIVES

BEAR ID. OR IDS. (BIARNEY) NO. 1:
> Near Godthaab, Greenland: Storm, Babcock, Hermannsson.
> Disko: Graah, Bruun, Thórdarson, Power.
> Off Baffin Land: J. T. Smith.
> Southeastern Baffin Land: Steensby.

HELLULAND (LAND OF FLAT STONES):
> Labrador and Newfoundland (two different regions) : Rafn.
> Northern Labrador: Steensby, Hovgaard, Dieserud, Hermannsson, Thórdarson, Curran.
> Labrador and Northern Newfoundland: C. H. L. Jones.
> Labrador as a whole: Packard, Markham, Grenfell, Wallace, Storm, Babcock, Bruun, Fischer.
> Newfoundland: Howley, Horsford, Gathorne-Hardy (preferably), Kohl. (Howley says "in neighborhood of Pt. Riche or Flower Cove.")

MARKLAND (FOREST-LAND):
> Southeast Labrador: Steensby, Hermannsson, Grenfell, Hovgaard, Fernald, Thórdarson.
> Southeast Labrador or Newfoundland: Dieserud.
> Newfoundland: Packard, Nansen, Storm, Babcock, Fischer.
> Nova Scotia: Rafn, Hovgaard, Horsford, Gathorne-Hardy, Kohl, Packard (doubtfully).
> East of Penobscot Bay, Me.: Goodwin.
> James Bay Region: Curran.

BEAR ISLAND (BIARNEY) NO. 2:
> Belle Isle: Thórdarson, Dieserud.
> Northern Peninsula of Newfoundland: Steensby, Hermannsson ("probably").
> Avalon Peninsula, Newfoundland: Babcock.

WONDER-STRANDS (FURDUSTRANDIR):
> Labrador: Fernald, Grenfell.
> South Coast of Labrador: Steensby, Hermannsson, Thórdarson.
> South of Sandwich Bay, Labrador: Hovgaard.
> East Coast of Cape Breton Island: Storm.
> East Coast of Nova Scotia: Babcock, C. H. Jones.
> East Coast of Nova Scotia between Cape North and St. Ann's Bay: Dieserud.
> Between York River and Old Orchard Beach, Me.: Goodwin.
> Coast of Cape Cod: Horsford.
> Outer Coast of Cape Cod and Barnstable Co.: Gathorne-Hardy.
> West Coast of Hudson Bay: Curran.

KEELNESS (KIALARNES):
> Point Vaches: Steensby (stated doubtfully).
> East Cape, Anticosti Island: Hermannsson.

Cape Gaspé, Quebec Province: Thórdarson.
Cape Breton, N. S.: Storm.
Cape North, Cape Breton Island: Babcock.
Cape North or Cape Egmont, Cape Breton Island: Dieserud.
Cape Small Point, Me.: Goodwin.
Cape Cod, Mass.: Horsford.

STREAMFIRTH (STRAUMFIORD):
Chaleur Bay, Quebec Province: Hermannsson.
Sandwich Bay, Labrador: Hovgaard.
St. Lawrence Estuary: Steensby.
Miramichi Bay, Cocagne Harbor, or Shediac Bay, N. B.: Thórdarson.
Bay of Fundy, N. S.: Babcock.
St. Mary Bay, N. S.: C. H. L. Jones.
Mira Bay, N. S.: Dieserud.
Strait of Canso or a neighboring inlet, N. S.: Storm.
Portsmouth Harbor, N. H.: Goodwin.
Chatham Harbor, Mass.: Horsford.
Buzzards Bay, Mass.: Rafn.
Long Island Sound: Gathorne-Hardy.

STREAM ISLE (STRAUMEY):
Hare Island in St. Lawrence Entrance. Steensby.
Heron Island in Chaleur Bay: Hermannsson.
Grand Manan in the Bay of Fundy: Babcock.
Scatari Island, N. S.: Dieserud.
Newcastle Island in Portsmouth Harbor: Goodwin.
Island of spit south of Chatham, Mass.: Horsford.
Martha's Vineyard: Rafn.
Fishers Island in Long Island Sound: Gathorne-Hardy.

WINELAND (VINLAND):
Part of Labrador: Fernald, Grenfell.
About Rivière du Sud, Quebec Province: Steensby.
Southern Nova Scotia: Storm, Fischer.
Nova Scotia not farther south than Halifax: Dieserud.
Sop's Arm on the Northeast Coast of Newfoundland: Hovgaard.
Miramichi Bay, N. B.: Howley.
East Coast of New England: Thórdarson.
Plymouth Harbor, Mass.: Goodwin.
Cape Cod Region: Kohl.
East and South Parts of Cape Cod: Packard.
Back Bay Region, Mass.: Horsford.
Vicinity of Cape Cod or Long Island Sound: C. H. L. Jones.
Mt. Hope Bay, R. I.: Rafn, Babcock.
Region of Great Lakes: Curran.
(Mythic): Nansen.

RIVER OR FIRTH NORTH OF KEELNESS:
St. Lawrence Entrance: Hermannsson, Thórdarson.

One of the small rivers flowing into Northumberland Strait: Babcock, Dieserud.

Kennebec River, Me.: Goodwin.

CROSS POINT (CROSSANES):

Pt. Alderton south of Boston Harbor, Mass.: Rafn.

South end of Georgetown Island, Me.: Goodwin.

In the bibliography at the end of this paper I have included only those works which have been referred to directly or indirectly. William H. Babcock and J. Fischer appended the titles of about 320 works to each of their respective publications. Besides the authorities included in my own list, which embraces only about 69 titles, I wish to make special acknowledgment to Dr. Harrison F. Lewis, Chief Federal Migratory Bird Officer of Ontario and Quebec Provinces, who has supplied me with some important information regarding the geography of the St. Lawrence region and the habits of the sea birds nesting there.

Let us see which of the identifications that have been attempted seem to stand up best under another examination of the material or whether in certain cases different ones might plausibly be suggested. The only sites which concern us and may be said to have been fixed beyond question are Ericsfiord and Heriulsfiord in Greenland (see page 6).

On leaving Ericsfiord Karlsefni is said to have voyaged first to the Western Settlement in the present Gothaab district, but as this lay in a direction contrary to his objective there has been much speculation among students as to his reason for doing so. It has been supposed that Gudrid, Karlsefni's wife, wished to visit a property she had inherited from her first husband which lay in Lysufiord, believed to be the present Ameralikfiord; that the voyagers wished to take advantage of more favorable winds and ocean currents; and possibly that they were aware of the narrowing of Davis Strait and the greater proximity of the American shores in that direction. It is known that Disko Island was called Bear Island and this has induced Bruun, Power, and Thórdarson to identify it with the Bear Island of the Saga, but most writers regard this as too far north. J. T. Smith suggests an island off Baffin Land, and Steensby inclines to view it as "a part of south-easterly Baffin Land." Hermannsson admits the possibility, mentioning specifically Resolution Island, but objects that the wording of the Saga assumes a previous knowledge of this island while it is intimated elsewhere that there was no knowledge among the Norsemen of the lands west of Davis Strait. Storm, Babcock, and Hermannsson therefore believe that it was some island or islands (one manuscript using the plural) off the Greenland coast near Godthaab (Brunn, 1918, p. 58; Power, 1892, pp. 175-176; Thórdarson, 1930, p. 15; Smith, 1839, map; Steensby, 1918, p. 34; Hermannsson, 1936, pp. 65-67; Babcock, 1913, pp. 54, 98). With this view I am inclined to agree, but the matter will probably never be settled. In any event it is of minor consequence.

Helluland is the first territory reached by Karlsefni known to have been west of Baffin Bay. The fact that this would be the most probable landfall for any vessel sailing southwest from Greenland, combined with the descriptions of the country as stony, without grass even, and with high "ice mountains" (Flat Island Book) upon it have led by far the greater number of investigators to identify it with Labrador or with some part of Labrador. The principal exceptions are the less conservative students who wish to extend Karlsefni's voyage as far to the south as possible and seek to make the descriptions square with Newfoundland. We should probably interpret "ice mountains" as "snowy mountains."

It is plain both from the documents and the name itself that Markland ("Forest-land") lay to the south of Helluland. Since forests begin in southern Labrador and extend southward indefinitely, theorizers have had a wide area of choice. Those who believe that the voyagers kept outside of Newfoundland have quite generally identified Markland with that island, but they have sometimes included southern Labrador on the supposition that the Strait of Belle Isle was unperceived and ignored. A few of the less conservative speculators, particularly those who place Helluland in Newfoundland, believe that Markland was Nova Scotia. Curran, who carries his explorers boldly through Hudson Strait into Hudson Bay, finds Markland in the James Bay region. Steensby and his followers, believing that Karlsefni entered the Gulf of St. Lawrence through the Strait of Belle Isle, confine Markland to southern Labrador (Steensby, 1918, pp. 42-47; Hermannsson, 1936, p. 59; Thórdarson, 1930, p. 21). Others have doubted, or discounted, this on the ground that the Labrador forest growth is small and is almost absent from the offshore islands and the headlands. The official map of Canadian forests (Atlas of Canada, pp. 17-18) shows, however, "densely wooded northern forest" between Hamilton Inlet and Sandwich Bay. H. G. Watkins (1930, p. 98) reports that—

southern Labrador is so thickly wooded that it is impossible to do any planetable work. Even the high hills are usually covered with trees, and for the most part it is an undulating country with no outstanding peaks.

As a result of exploration in the peninsula, A. P. Low (1896, p. 31L) says:

The forest is continuous over the southern part of the peninsula to between latitudes 52° and 54°, the only exceptions being the summits of rocky hills and the outer islands of the Atlantic coast. To the northward of latitude 53°, the higher hills are treeless, woods being only found about the margins of small lakes and in the valleys of the rivers. Trees also decrease in size until, on the southern shores of Ungava Bay, they disappear altogether.

Packard (1891, pp. 118, 125, 140) reports of the shores of Anse-au-Loup in the Strait of Belle Isle that they seemed to be "well wooded." Again:

The lumber for these shanties [in Pitt's Arm of Temple Bay] had evidently, by the piles of sawdust near by, been sawn upon the spot and taken from the Labradorian forest of firs near at hand, which measured twelve inches through at the butt, and were about twenty feet high.

At the head of a bay near Cape St. Michaels was "quite a forest of spruce." From W. A. Stearns (1884, pp. 98, 117) I quote the following:

From the entrance of the bay [of Bonne Esperance] then, as I have said, we caught a view of the Indian mishwaps [dwellings], backed by the verdure of slopes, hills, ravines, ridges, and the various contour of a most uneven background in the profile of the evergreen spruce tops,—which low shrub is everywhere abundant outside as is the large tree inland. . . . Those who can obtain wood near by without the necessity of going into the interior up the river, and rafting it down, as many of them do, content themselves with a smaller article, and continue to make clearings in the low spruce and fir about their own place. The majority of this wood varies from four to six and even seven inches in diameter, while the trees are rarely over fifteen feet in height.

Greenland visitors to this coast were not likely to be too demanding as to the size of trees or extent of forest in a country better blessed then their own.

The Flat Island Book in its narrative of Leif's voyage adds to the description of Markland that "there were broad stretches of white sand where they went." Unless this is reminiscent of the Wonderstrands, we may find it in the sandy shores reported around Sandwich Bay, but I incline to the former view.

An island off the coast of Markland was given the name of Bear Island from the circumstance of their having killed a bear upon it, and this is therefore Bear Island No. 2. Those who think that Karlsefni passed through the Strait of Belle Isle identify this either with the northern peninsula of Newfoundland or with Belle Isle itself, and Dieserud holds the latter view although he carries the explorers south outside of Newfoundland. Others of this school seem to avoid theorizing on the point except Babcock (1913, pp. 108-109), who suggests an identification with Avalon Peninsula which he supposes was taken to be an island.

Differences of opinion among investigators become more marked when they take up points beyond Markland, including the Wonderstrands, the cape named Keelness (Kialarnes), Streamfirth (Straumfiord), Stream Isle (Straumey), the river or inlet in which Thorvald was killed, and Hop or Wineland. The voyagers made two lengthy stops during this part of their journey, one at Streamfirth and the other at Hop or Wineland. We will discuss the location of these in order, but it is to be noted at the very beginning that the Flat Island Book seems to confuse them, identifying both with Wineland, and therefore we must depend more than ever upon the Saga in our discussion of the whereabouts of the former. Here our more careful students fall into two schools, one maintaining that Karlsefni kept east of Newfoundland, that the Wonder-strands were on the outer coasts of Cape Breton Island and Nova Scotia, one or both, and Streamfirth was either the Bay of Fundy as Babcock (1913, p. 118) has it, or some bay in southern Nova Scotia—Mira Bay, thinks Dieserud (1901, p. 12), St. Mary Bay according to Jones and Raddall (1934, p. 106). According to the second school, Karlsefni entered the Gulf of St. Lawrence through the Strait of Belle Isle, the Wonderstrands were on the south coast of Labrador, and Streamfirth was the estuary of St. Lawrence River, Chaleur Bay, or one of the bays south of the latter.

Strong arguments can be brought forward in favor of each of these theories, and it happens, unfortunately, that the two versions of the Saga differ just at this point sufficiently to support both. The Hauk's Book version informs us that, after leaving Markland—

they sailed southward along the land for a long time, and came to a cape; the land lay upon the starboard; there were long strands and sandy banks there. They rowed to the land and found upon the cape there the keel of a ship, and they called it there Kialarnes (Keelness); they also called the strands Furdustrandir (Wonder-strands) because they were so long to sail by. Then the country became indented with bays, and they steered their ships into a bay. . . . .

The second version is as follows:

When 2 dœgr had elapsed [after leaving Markland], they descried land, and they sailed off this land; there was a cape to which they came. They beat into the wind along this coast, having the land upon the starboard side. This was a bleak coast, with long and sandy shores. They went ashore in boats, and found the keel of a ship, so they called it Keelness there; they likewise gave a name to the strands, and called them Wonder-strands, because they were long to sail by.

The first version gives us to understand that the Wonder-strands, including Keelness, were on land continuous with Markland and there was no break in the coast. That is what we should expect if Karlsefni entered the Strait of Belle Isle and kept on along the southern coast of Labrador. According to the second version, however, there was open sea or a broad inlet between Markland and the Wonder-strands, and this favors the Nova Scotia theory. It would not, of course, take 2 dœgr to pass the Strait of Belle Isle, but in order to reach Nova Scotia from Newfoundland it would have been necessary to cross Cabot Strait and this might well have taken the time indicated. Although confounded with the later stay at Hop, the events which took place in the region we are studying are covered by the Flat Island Book in a few sentences, and these may be interpreted to favor both theories. After leaving Markland we are told:

They returned to the ship forthwith, and sailed away upon the main with northeast winds, and were out two "dœgr" before they sighted land. They sailed toward this land, and came to an island which lay to the northward off the land.

The "2 'dœgr'" may be quoted in confirmation of the second version of the Saga. It happens, however, that in describing Markland just before this, the Flat Island Book, besides stating that it was "a level wooded land," adds "there were broad stretches of white sand, where they went, and the land was level by the sea." This happens to be the only mention of sandy beaches in connection with Markland, but in the confused state of the Flat Island narrative and remembering that the Wonder-strands are described in the first version of the Saga as continuous with Markland, one can use this to confirm the topography of that version.

The Nova Scotia theory derives considerable strength from what is said of the expedition of Thorhall from Streamfirth "in search of Wineland" and Karlsefni's subsequent search for him. According to the Saga, Thorhall "sailed away to the northward past Wonder-strands and Keelness, intending to cruise to the westward around the cape." It would appear from the ditty supposed to have been composed by Thorhall on this occasion that his real object was to return home, but an intention to hunt for Wineland might have been his excuse, and if the explorers crossed Cabot Strait on their way to Nova Scotia without having entered it, the possibility that Wineland was to be found by sailing through it was plausible. In his search for

Thorhall next summer Karlsefni pursued the course that the former was supposed to have taken. He and his companions—

sailed to the northward around Keelness, and then bore to the westward, having land to the larboard. The country there was a wooded wilderness, as far as they could see, with scarcely an open space, and when they had journeyed a considerable distance, a river flowed down from the east toward the west. They sailed into the mouth of the river and lay to by the southern bank.

Westward-flowing streams are scarce along the northeast coast of America but there are some flowing into Northumberland Strait that might answer to the description, and Thorvald's enthusiasm over the region they entered, in the Flat Island Book, would be justified. At the other end of Nova Scotia the Bay of Fundy with its renowned tides would fit ideally with what is said of Streamfirth, but I doubt whether the tides on the outer coast of Nova Scotia are sufficiently conspicuous to encourage us to choose St. Mary Bay or Mira Bay. If the Bay of Fundy was Streamfirth, we could find a bird island in one of the Tusket Islands but hardly in Grand Manan as Babcock (1913, pp. 118-120) suggested.

A weak point in the theory is the supposition that our voyagers passed all the way round the irregular east and south coasts of Newfoundland without comment. The most serious objection, however, arises when one attempts to identify the Wonder-strands with the modern topography. A long, relatively straight, and to some extent sandy, coast is indicated. This excludes the coast of Newfoundland and compels us to seek for it on the east coasts of Cape Breton Island and Nova Scotia. This is a stumbling block even if we agree with Dieserud, as does the writer, that Wonder-strands does not necessarily mean Wonder-sands and we need not look for long sandy beaches like those of New Jersey or even southern Maine and New Hampshire. Dieserud (1901, p. 12) is able to cite the existence of one sandy beach of at least a mile in length in Ingonish Bay and places Wonder-strands between Cape North and St. Ann's Bay on the northern projection of Cape Breton Island, but that is some distance from the long, straight coast we are led to search for which would begin at Cape Breton, and it seems hardly extensive enough to answer to the language used. Babcock (1913, pp. 112-117) sought a different solution by supposing that the configuration of the east coast of Nova Scotia had been radically altered since A. D. 1000 by the rising of the land. He was in error in supposing that the land is rising. It is actually sinking (Dr. Lewis, personal communication). But this need not destroy the force of the theory if it can be shown that when the land was higher, the coast line was in keeping with the description in the Saga. Nevertheless, it would not seem that men from Greenland who had recently passed along the Labrador coast would describe that of Nova Scotia as "bleak" as does one version of the Saga. A minor criticism is furnished by the fact that the Flat Island Book seems to say that they sailed west into Streamfirth, whereas the Bay of Fundy extends from southwest to northeast. In view, however, of the uncertain value of so many Flat Island Book statements this must not be overrated. On the other hand, I have omitted one argument in Nova Scotia's favor which will appear when we come to take up the problem presented by Wineland.

What may be called the Labrador theory of the location of the Wonder-strands was first proposed by Steensby, and it has been accepted by a number of the best subsequent students such as Hermannsson and Thórdarson (Steensby, 1918, pp. 42-47; Hermannsson, 1936, p. 59; Thórdarson, 1930, p. 21). It derives its great strength from the fact that the southern Labrador coast is relatively straight, long, and "bleak," but particularly because one can here point to a considerable number of long sandy beaches. Dr. Lewis has kindly supplied me with data regarding these which are as follows.

	Miles
Blanc Sablon Bay	1
Anse des Dunes, Bradore Bay	1
Sandy Island, St. Augustin	1
Vicinity of mouth of Netagamiu River	8
Kegaska Bay to Natashquan	31
Vicinity of mouth of Agwanus River	9
Clearwater Point to west of Eskimo Point	9
Mingan River to Magpie	23
Matamek to Bay of Seven Islands	26

The first considerable stretch of sand occurs just east of Cape Whittle, where the trend of the coast as one enters the Bay of St. Lawrence changes from southwest to west, and from Kegaska Bay on, sand beaches are fairly numerous and long. East of Netagamiu River the coast is generally bold, rocky, and desolate. I quote the following from Packard (1891, p. 63) regarding this part of the coast:

As we approach land no capes run out to greet us, or sheltered harbor opens its arms to embrace. An uninterrupted line of coast confronts the gulf. In one place alone is the intense monotony of the outline relieved by the hills of Bradore, where the coast sweeps round fifteen miles to the eastward, and the Strait [of Belle Isle] widens out.

The total distance from the eastern entrance of the Strait of Belle Isle to Cape Whittle is about 225 miles, and from Cape Whittle to Seven Islands 280 miles, 98 of this latter consisting of sand beaches. Undoubtedly this fits the description of the Sagas better than any other location that has been suggested and that has any probability in its favor.

We have considerable difficulty, however, in determining the location of Keelness, because the narratives leave us in some doubt whether it was at the near or far end of the Wonder-strands as the voyagers approached it or whether it lay in an intermediate position. Those who place Wonder-strands on the south coast of Labrador have uniformly located it at the western end because they have thought it necessary to identify the western wooded land visited by Karlsefni with the estuary of the St. Lawrence, though there has been no agreement among them as to the identity of the cape. Steensby, somewhat doubtfully, suggested Point Vaches at the mouth of the Saguenay River, but this is by no means conspicuous, nor is it easy to see how an explorer from the south could pass around it and turn west. Here Steensby has felt compelled to resort to an elaborate reconstruction of the narrative which is labored and has been accepted by no one else. Hermannsson proposed the East Cape of Anticosti Island, his theory being that the voyagers sighted it as they passed westward along the Labrador coast, cut across to it under the impression that it was the south headland of a bay, and from there entered Chaleur Bay which he identifies as Streamfirth. On leaving in search of Thorhall he thinks Karlsefni rounded the same cape as being a known landmark and then turned west into the St. Lawrence estuary unaware of the shorter route between Anticosti and Gaspé. Thórdarson, however, esteems it incredible that Karlsefni's company who had, according to the narrative, spent all their first summer exploring the country, should have been unaware of this wide passage. He accordingly identifies Keelness with Cape Gaspé but otherwise agrees with Hermannsson as to the location of the region of the Unipeds visited by Karlsefni (Hermannsson, 1936, p. 68; Thórdarson, 1930, pp. 25, 36). Thórdarson's emendation seems logical, and it has the same strength as the Nova Scotia theory in being able to point to a western inlet for exploration by parties in search of Wineland—in this case the St. Lawrence estuary rather than the entire Gulf of St. Lawrence. Indeed, Steensby (1918, pp. 64-76) locates Hop higher up this very estuary but thereby is left without any proper explanation of the region covered by Karlsefni in his search for Thorhall, since this lay to the north of Streamfirth, while Hop, from which he had recently come, was far to the south.

One difficulty with the theories of Hermannsson and Thórdarson is that they fail to indicate an inlet corresponding sufficiently well with the Streamfirth of the Sagas. Chaleur Bay is ideal from the point of view of climate and the presence of pasture lands suitable for the Norsemen's cattle, but although the tides rise 10 feet near its head, they are much lower at its entrance, and the currents are not conspicuous. Heron Island, which is suggested as the Stream Island of the explorers, is near the head of the bay, whereas the narratives place Stream Island close to the entrance, and I am informed by Dr. Lewis that it is too large for a bird rookery. The latter criticism would also apply to Miscou Island at the mouth of Chaleur Bay. On the other hand Miramichi Bay, Cocagne Harbor, and Shediac Bay, suggested by Thórdarson (1930, pp. 37-38) are not particularly noted for their currents. Those in Shediac Bay are reported to be "weak," and although there is considerable current at times in Miramichi Bay, the tides rise only 4 to 6 feet. Nor are the islands at the mouth of these bays suitable for bird nesting places. Moreover, as Thorhall indicates in his ditty, Streamfirth was close to Wonder-strands. Both of these thories also suffer from the fact that they separate Keelness farther from Wonder-strands than the narratives warrant. The first version of the Saga speaks of the cape before it mentions the strands, the second version speaks of them together; Thorhall and his men "sailed away to the northward" past Wonder-strands and Keelness, intending to cruise to the westward around the cape, and Karlsefni, when in search of him, is said to have rounded the cape and voyaged west, although here nothing is said of Wonder-strands. The two last references imply that the cape was at the extreme eastern end of the strands, and that one could steer west immediately after passing it, but this may not have been the case, since the first version of the Saga says that after leaving Markland "they sailed southward along the land for a long time" before coming to the cape, and the wording of the second version is not averse to such an interpretation, while both apparently intimate that if Keelness was not on a sandy coast, sand was not far away. I would suggest as a solution that Keelness may have been at or near Cape Whittle, that the coast along which the Hauk's Book narrative says they sailed "for a long time" after leaving Markland was that part of the Labrador coast east of Cape Whittle. Since this section of the coast trends southwest, the statement that they were following it "southward" would not be too much out of line. An exact identification of this cape I shall not attempt, merely placing it somewhere between Netagamiu River and Natashkwan Point. It is true that the later references to Keelness would lead us to suppose that navigators could turn directly west after rounding it, but we do not have to interpret such statements too literally. If we could be sure that Thorhall was genuinely bent on sailing westward after passing Keelness, the fact that he was driven to Ireland shows, on the Labrador theory, that he passed through the Strait of Belle Isle in pursuit of his object, for we cannot believe that he was driven through that strait against his will. This, it may be observed, applies still more forcibly to the theories of Steensby, Hermannsson, and Thórdarson, since, if we accept them, we have to assume that Thorhall was driven across the entire expanse of the Gulf of St. Lawrence and through the Strait of Belle Isle or Cabot Strait, and across the Atlantic on top of that. Our only escape from this would be to suppose that Thorhall did not intend to turn westward but made for the open ocean.

Our documentary sources give no warrant for the assumption that Keelness was separated from the Wonder-strands by an inlet. If Keelness was at or near Cape Whittle, we must look for the river or inlet into which Karlsefni sailed in search of Thorhall somewhere east of it, and unless we can identify it with the estuary of some river like the St. Augustin, we shall have to suppose that they reached Sandwich Bay or Hamilton Inlet. Probably one would not think of this as a region to excite the admiration Thorvald is said to have expressed, but it differs from the surrounding parts of Labrador in harboring a dense forest, and in spite of the length of the voyage required to reach it, it is not to be excluded as a possibility in locating the land of the Unipeds. It suffers in our eyes in comparison with the St. Lawrence estuary or Nova Scotia but may have made a different impression on the mind of a Greenlander.

As opposed to the attempted placement of Keelness by Steensby, Hermannsson, and Thórdarson, the Nova Scotia theorizers can point to a very satisfactory Keelness at the northern end of Cape Breton Island, and in addition to that to a very satisfactory Streamfirth in the Bay of Fundy (Babcock, 1913, p. 110), but unless they can resurrect out of the geological past a coast line on the seaward side of Nova Scotia much more in keeping with what we are told of Wonder-strands than anything found there today, the theory is fatally defective.

Indeed, the southern coast of Labrador seems to be the only one in the entire St. Lawrence region that in any way fits the documentary descriptions. Moreover, it has all the strength of the Nova Scotia theory in being immediately connected with a tidal inlet corresponding to Streamfirth whether we identify it with the strait north of Anticosti Island or look for it higher up in the St. Lawrence estuary. Jacques Cartier (Biggar, 1924, p. 74) gives testimony to the strength of tides in the former in the record of his first voyage. His longboats were sent ahead of the vessels to row up to the head of Anticosti on its northern side, but—

when we had rowed along the said coast for some two hours, the tide began to turn and came against us from the west so violently that it was impossible to make a stone's throw of headway with thirteen oars. And we deemed it advisable to leave the long-boats, with part of our men to stand guard over them, and for ten or twelve of us to go along the shore as far as that cape where we found that the coast began to turn off towards the south-west [i.e., to North Point on Anticosti]. When we had seen this, we made our way back to our long-boats and returned on board the ships, which were still under sail, hoping always to make headway; but they had drifted more than four leagues to leeward from the spot where we had left them.

The tides in the St. Lawrence estuary are stronger yet, attaining their maximum at the mouth of the Saguenay where they reach a velocity at times of 6 or 7 knots an hour (St. Lawrence Pilot, 1924, p. 411).

Either of these locations would fit the statements in the narratives which give us to understand that Streamfirth was near the Wonder-strands and that it was entered immediately after passing them. The Saga says: "Then the country became indented with bays, and they steered their ships into a bay." On reading this some have supposed that the voyagers passed a number of bays and chose to enter one of them. I think, however, that the first part of the sentence is merely introductory to the second. They had been sailing along what seemed to them an open coast, and afterwards came to a part of it where bays began and they sailed into one of them which we may equally well suppose was the first.

The Saga continues:

There was an island out at the mouth of the bay, about which there were strong currents, wherefore they called it Straumey [Stream Isle]. There were so many birds there, that it was scarcely possible to step between the eggs. They sailed through the firth, and called it Straumfiord [Streamfirth], and carried their cargoes ashore from the ships, and established themselves there. They had brought with them all kinds of live-stock. It was a fine country there. There were mountains thereabouts. They occupied themselves exclusively with the exploration of the country. They remained there during the winter, and they had taken no thought for this during the summer. The fishing began to fail and they began to fall short of food.

Thorhall the Huntsman exerts his pagan charms and a whale is found, but the colonists are made sick by eating its flesh, they throw all away into the sea, and appeal to God, whereupon:

The weather then improved, and they could now row out to fish, and thenceforward they had no lack of provisions, for they could hunt game on the land, gather eggs on the island, and catch fish from the sea.

Bird islands are so common in the St. Lawrence region that it would be impossible to find the one here described even though the identity of Streamfirth is correctly established. One of the narratives, instead of speaking of birds, mentions specifically eider ducks. Steensby seeks to identify the bird island with Hare Island which lies just above the mouth of the Saguenay but Dr. Lewis tells me that it is too large to be a favorite resort of nesting birds.

While the estuary of the St. Lawrence corresponds very satisfactorily with the Streamfirth of the narratives, we must assume that, if the Norse were there, they did not carry their explorations far enough toward the head of the Gulf to discover that a mighty river poured into it. Some question may be raised as to the possibility of carrying cattle over the winter in that section, but this part of the Gulf region certainly has a more favorable climate than is commonly supposed. The Canadian zone of vegetation succeeds the Hudsonian here and extends up along the coast to Cape Whittle, while the southern forest area passes beyond Pte. des Monts (Atlas of Canada, 1915, pp. 17, 18). The relative mildness of the Mingan section, for instance, is thus described by Stearns (1884, pp. 256-258):

On the mainland, or Mingan proper, contrary to what might be expected from the appearance of the island opposite, an entirely different formation exists. Nowhere along the coast, for a considerable distance at least, does a rock of any size appear, either in place or loose as bowlder, stone, or pebble. Strange to say, as will be shown further on, the rocky precipices, or rather steps of the rapids in Mingan river, some three miles from its mouth, seem to be the first indications of rock formation in this locality, while these are simply the eastern and southeastern boundary of a tremendous mass of high rocky ground that extends inland for miles, perhaps thousands of miles.

The coast and its beach, as the whole country to the rocks inland, is everywhere low and sandy. On the beach itself the sand is dense and very fine. Farther in shore there is a very scant, occasional streak of low vegetation where are pastured a few heads of cattle and goats that graze on the lawns, here and there, where they can find food. A few acres of good grass are fenced in, and this supplies an excellent feed for the animals during the winter, which here is neither so long nor so severe as is usually the case farther north, at

Bonne Esperance even. From Mingan west to Long Point, a distance of about six miles, this low sand beach extends almost without a single rock, I believe, while the east beach is entirely of sand. The river itself passes through a ridge of this same material which forms a high bank on the left and a low one on the right, as one passes inland, while the whole land rises directly from the sea then falls in a northeasterly direction, and the trend of greatest height, here, as nearly everywhere along this part of the coast, is in a northwesterly direction. In the background, the distant hills rise to the height of at least a thousand feet, while dim outlines of others, of perhaps greater height, appear in the horizon. This is the picture whose charming outline at once attracts and captivates one upon entering the harbor of this sequestered little spot. . . .

At the mouth of both rivers [the Mingan and Romaine] are shallows and accumulations filling the water with ridges that control strongly the current at this point. These sand bars are constantly shifting, while in places they have overrun each other and piled up small islands of sand which becoming overgrown with grass or scant vegetation have become the nesting places of gulls and ducks, thus supplying the people with birds and eggs in large numbers whenever they are desired. Following up the river [Mingan] you will find sand and sand banks on either hand, and extending, with scant vegetation, far inland. . . . .

"From the shore [at the mouth of Mingan River] we could see the summit of Mt. St. John's, lying some fifteen miles inland in a northwesterly direction, which mountain is said to be a little over fourteen hundred feet in height. Directly inland the country is said to rise in successive steps—if one might use the word in this connection,—to what is termed the "height of land," some five hundred miles inland, where a chain of mountains, peculiar to the whole lower St. Lawrence region, and northerly Quebec, with peaks varying from one to three thousand feet in height, continues in an eastern trend towards the sea, which it reaches at the extremity of the Labrador peninsula, near Ivucktoke, or Hamilton Inlet.

Here we have sufficient feed for a few cattle at least, bird islands, strong tides, and a background of mountains. A place possessing somewhat similar advantages is Seven Islands, farther west, a former Indian gathering place, and there are other places suitable for settlement such as the Greenlanders were attempting higher up on both sides of the river. I think there is no doubt that we are in the immediate region of Streamfirth even if we cannot carry our identification any closer.

In transferring the sites of Wonder-strands, Keelness, Stream Isle, and Streamfirth from Newfoundland and Nova Scotia to points inside the Gulf of St. Lawrence, Steensby performed a distinct service to all students of the Wineland voyages, but when he goes on to place Wineland in the same region, only farther up toward the mouth of the river, like Hermannsson and Thórdarson, I fail to follow him. Carried far enough it would bring the voyagers into a wild-grape country but, at the same time, to a certain knowledge of the great river, and of this the Sagas contain no trace. Moreover, Steensby does not seem to have noticed that such a location would be in violent contradiction with what is said about Leif's discovery of Wineland in the Saga of Eric the Red which Steensby accepts as authoritative. For it tells us that he came upon that region after having been tossed about for a long time on the North Atlantic when he was on his way from Norway to Greenland, and it is evident that he would not have been driven through Cabot Strait and deep into the Gulf of St. Lawrence, or of his own volition would have voyaged thither. This objection would, indeed, be removed if we accept the story of Leif's discovery of Wineland substantially as it is given in the Flat Island Book, but there are other serious difficulties, one being the failure of the Norse to discover the St. Lawrence as noted above and another the short distance between Steensby's sites at Hare Island and the mouth of the Rivière du Sud, where he places Hop. This is less than 90 miles, far from sufficient to require a voyage that could be described as occupying "a long time." Taking advantage of the tide, as they certainly would have, a few hours would have been sufficient.

Attempts to locate Streamfirth other than those considered have little to recommend them. They are usually too far from the probable cruising radius of the Norse explorers or present only isolated and superficial resemblances to the regions described by our authorities.

This introduces us to a general consideration of the southernmost stopping place of the Norse explorers, Wineland itself. It has been confounded frequently with the region of Streamfirth very largely because it was so confounded by the compilers of the Flat Island Book, but the distinction is clearly indicated in the Saga of Eric the Red. Thus we are told that Thorhall went from Streamfirth "in search of Wineland" while Karlsefni voyaged south for the same purpose. It is true that *after* Karlsefni's return to Streamfirth we read that they came upon five Skrellings, among whom were two boys whom they made captive and from whom they obtained information regarding their people, and that this episode begins with the words "when they sailed away from Wineland," but it has not been observed that the whole section is an interpolation and probably an attempt to elaborate the episode of the five Skrellings whom they met and murdered when they were on their way from Wineland to Streamfirth.

Adequate reasons have already been given, I believe, for rejecting Steensby's theory of the location of Wineland.

We are not given the distance from Streamfirth to Hop (Wineland) but are merely told that in order to reach it "they sailed for a long time." How long that might be was left to the imagination of the reader, and imaginations have been busy with it ever since. But we have seen that when (or if) they sailed from the entrance of the Strait of Belle Isle to Cape Whittle, a distance of about 225 miles, it took them, according to one narrative "a long time," and according to another 2 dœgr. The Wonder-strands, a somewhat longer stretch of coast according to our theory, were "long to sail by."

If Streamfirth was the Bay of Fundy or anywhere in that neighborhood, we would naturally look for Wineland in New England, and a time period of 2 dœgr, the period of passage mentioned in the Flat Island Book, might very well bring us there but the accuracy of the scource is not to be counted on and according to various authorities a dœgr might mean anything from 50 miles to 150 or 200. If Streamfirth was in the St. Lawrence estuary or Chaleur Bay the distance covered would be nearer 900 miles, and our 2 dœgr would not carry us farther than Northumberland Strait.

The early, widely accepted theory as to the location of Wineland, fathered by Rafn, placed it in Mount Hope Bay, R. I., on the very slender possibility that the word "Hop," applied by Karlsefni to the lake or lakelike expansion of the river where they set up their cabins, had somehow survived into modern times. Babcock (1913, p. 137) accepted this theory, but, as in the case of the Wonder-strands, had to suppose considerable geological change during the last 900 years in order to establish a resemblance between the Mount Hope Bay of today and the Hop described in the Sagas. Instead of a single entrance with offshore bars, there are two deep-water entrances into this bay, and instead of one river flowing into it, there are four. The U. S. Coast Pilot for this section (U. S. Coast and Geodetic Survey, U. S. Coast Pilot, 1927, pp. 91, 105) says:

There are two approaches by water to this bay, one through Sakonnet River and the other through the Eastern Passage of Narragansett Bay. The former is little used [but "is good for a depth of 20 feet (6.1 m.) to Mount Hope Bay, a distance of 12 miles"]; the latter [approach]. . . . has a depth of over 6 fathoms (11 m.) in the channel until in the bay.

Of the four rivers entering the bay, the principal is Taunton River.

Before continuing this discussion, however, it will be well to quote those passages from the narratives upon which we must depend for any attempted identifications. First, from the Saga of Eric the Red:

It is now told of Karlsefni, that he cruised southward off the coast [from Streamfirth], with Snorri and Biarni, and their people. They sailed for a long time, and until they came at last to a river, which flowed down from the land into a lake, and so into the sea. There were great bars at the mouth of the river, so that it could only be entered at the height of the flood-tide. Karlsefni and his men sailed into the mouth of the river, and called it there Hop [a small land-locked bay]. They found self-sown wheat fields on the land there, wherever there were hollows, and wherever there was hilly ground, there were vines. Every brook there was full of fish. They dug pits on the shore where the tide rose highest, and when the tide fell, there were halibut in the pits. There were great numbers of animals of all kinds in the woods. . . . No snow came there, and all of their live-stock lived by grazing.

The woods were near their dwellings as is proved by the fact that a bull frightened visiting natives away by running out of the woods, by the fact that one of the natives tested a Norse ax on a tree during the battle between the two parties, and by the fact that the Norse when attacked "fled into the forest."

When the Norsemen were put to flight by the Skrellings, they fled "up along the river bank" and "did not pause, until they came to certain jutting crags," giving us incidentally a topographic note.

After visiting the "land of the Unipeds" where Thorvald was killed, Karlsefni and his companions—

concluded that the mountains of Hop, and those which they had now found, formed one chain, and this appeared to be so because they were about an equal distance removed from Streamfirth, in either direction.

This seems to establish the existence of mountains in sight of Hop even if it was not in a mountainous country.

From the Flat Island Book we glean the following: After some details which evidently belong to the Streamfirth period confounded with the Wineland visit, it continues—

At ebb-tide there were broad reaches of shallow water there, and they ran their ship aground there, and it was a long distance from the ship to the ocean; yet were they so anxious to go ashore that they could not wait until the tide should rise under their ship, but hastened to the land, where a certain river flows out from a lake. As soon as the tide rose beneath their ship, however, they took the boat and rowed to the ship, which they conveyed up the river, and so into the lake, where they cast anchor and carried their hammocks ashore from the ship, and built themselves booths there. They afterwards determined to establish themselves there for the winter, and they accordingly built a large house. There was no lack of salmon there either in the river or in the lake, and larger salmon than they had ever seen before. The country thereabouts seemed to be possessed of such good qualities that cattle would need no fodder there during the winters. There was no frost there in the winters, and the grass withered but little. The days and nights there were of more nearly equal length than in Greenland or Iceland. On the shortest day of winter the sun was up between "eyktarstad" and "dagmalastad."

Grapes were soon discovered by the German Tyrker, and they returned to Greenland with a cargo of grapes, vines, and timber.

During Thorvald's supposed visit to Wineland a few men took the afterboat and explored the western coast the first summer.

They found it a fair, well-wooded country; it was but a short distance from the woods to the sea, and [there were] white sands, as well as great numbers of islands and shallows. They found neither dwelling of man nor lair of beast; but in one of the westerly isles, they found a wooden building for the shelter of grain. They found no other trace of human handiwork.

Thorvald also returned to Greenland with grapes and wood.

Karlsefni caused trees to be felled, and to be hewed into timbers, wherewith to load his ship, and the wood was placed upon a cliff to dry. They gathered somewhat of all of the valuable products of the land, grapes, and all kinds of game and fish, and other good things.

The Skrellings come through the woods, and the scene of battle was arranged by Karlsefni so as to have "the lake upon one side, and the forest upon the other." In preparation for this struggle 10 men were to show themselves upon "the cape." Karlsefni, like Leif and Thorvald, carries "vines and grapes" back to Greenland, but also peltries. Freydis carries "all the products of the land" back with her, but these are not enumerated.

In brief, at Hop was a lake with a river running through it or a lake-like expansion in a river, but it was so near the ocean that we do not know whether the water in it was salt or fresh. At the mouth of the river there were bars upon which the Norse vessels grounded at low tide, but at high tide they were able to pass over them into the lake. As we are told of the grounding only when our explorers first arrived, it is possible that there may have been a deeper channel which they missed. The region was thoroughly wooded. If the shelters erected there were not actually in the forest, the forest was close by, and some distance farther up the river, apparently not very far, was higher land described in the relations as "crags." From a later entry in the Saga it seems that there were mountains in sight.

If the account of that expedition "along the western coast" by Thorvald's men is to be relied upon, a similar coast, characterized by bars and sand islands, extended beyond Hop. To many writers this has suggested the southeastern shores of Massachusetts, and undoubtedly the southeastern coast of New England is one of those on which the narratives would lead us to look for Hop in spite of our rejection of Rafn's theory.

An inspection of the coast survey charts between Portland, Me., and New Haven, Conn., has yielded the following estuaries with inner expansions that might be regarded as lakes:

Scarboro River, Me., 5 feet over the bar at mean low tide; depth inside not given.

Hampton River, N. H., 3 feet over the bar; 20 feet inside.

Entrance of Merrimack River, Mass., 9 feet over the bar according to small-scale map, and 16½ on large-scale map, but the U. S. Coast Pilot says that the bar shifts and that the depth of water over it at mean low tide varies from 9 to 12 feet. The depth inside is 10-11 feet until one gets to Newburyport, when it is 12 to 18 feet.

Parker River and Plum Island Sound, Mass., 6 feet over the bar; 20 feet inside.

Essex River, Mass., 8 feet over the bar; 19 feet inside. ,

Barnstable Harbor, Mass., 5 feet over the bar; 19 feet inside.

Nauset Harbor, Mass., 6 feet over the bar; inside depth not given.

Chatham Harbor, Mass., 5 feet over the bar; 14 feet inside.

Mashpee River, Mass., 3 feet over the bar; 12 feet inside.

Slocums River, Mass., 2 feet over the bar; 7-8 feet inside.

The following information regarding these inlets is extracted from the U. S. Coast Pilot guide:

Spurwink and Scarboro Rivers, on the north side of the bight, can be entered only by small craft at half tide or higher with a smooth sea. They are seldom entered. [P. 211.]

Hampton Harbor, or Hampton River, a shallow stream used only by very small local craft, lies 1½ miles southwestward of Great Boars Head. The entrance is not safe for strangers. [P. 225.]

The entrance (of Newburyport Harbor, chart 331) is obstructed by a shifting bar, with 9 to 12 feet (2.7 to 3.7 m.) over it (according to the condition of the bar), which is dangerous to cross in heavy weather . . . . Jetties with an opening 1,000 feet wide between the ends have been built from both points at the entrance out to the bar. [P.225.]

Plum Island Sound (chart 1206) "is the approach to several small rivers and villages and is frequented by many small craft. Vessels seldom enter. It had a depth in 1926 of about 5 feet (1.5 m.) at low water across the bar."—Plum Island River "is bare at low water."—"Parker River, emptying into the north end of Plum Island Sound from westward, has a depth of about 5 feet (1.5 m.) in a very narrow channel to a fixed bridge at Newberry Old Town, 1¾ miles above the entrance. . . The river is navigable by small craft for several miles above Newberry Old Town, but is little used." [Pp. 228-229.]

Essex Bay and River (Chart 243) lie midway between Ipswich and Annisquam Lighthouses. The entrance is over a shifting bar, over which a depth of about 3 or 4 feet (0.9 to 1.2 m.) can be carried at low water through a narrow buoyed channel. The river is navigable to the town of Essex, 4 miles above its mouth, through a narrow dredged channel about 6 feet (1.8 m.) deep at low water. Vessels of 12-foot draft (3.7 m.), with local knowledge have been taken over the bar to an anchorage inside the entrance. [P. 229.]

Barnstable Harbor. . . . It is used by many local fishing boats but is seldom entered by strangers. The entrance is obstructed by a shifting bar with about 6 feet (1.8 m.) over it at low water. The Harbor is nearly filled by flats and shoals, which also extend 2 miles off the entrance from the shore eastward of the lighthouse. . . Few vessels enter the harbor, the greatest draft being 12 feet (3.7 m.). . . . After crossing the bar the channel has a depth of about 8 feet (2.4 m.) for 3 miles to within ⅛ mile of the wharf at Barnstable. [P. 293.]

Nauset Harbor. . . . The entrance is practically bare at low water and is used only by small local craft at high water. Strangers should never attempt to enter. [Atlantic Coast, Section B, Cape Cod to Sandy Hook, p. 35.]

Chatham Bar, the northern entrance to Chatham. . . The channel over the bar to the town of Chatham had a depth of about 3½ feet (1.1 m.) at low water in 1925, but is subject to frequent changes, and the buoys at the entrance can not be depended on to lead in the best water. The channel is used only by small local craft with a smooth sea and is not safe for strangers. The large shoal bay northward of the entrance is seldom entered. [Ibid.]

Mashpee River is not mentioned in the Coast Pilot Guide, but Poponesset Bay into which it flows is said to be "used only by local oyster boats." The entrance is narrow and unmarked, dredged to 60 feet wide and 6 feet (1.8 m.) deep. The entrance channel is subject to shoaling, and in 1925 was good for a draft of only 3 feet (0.9 m). [Ibid.]

Slocums River is evidently of slight importance because the name does not appear either in the Coast Pilot Guide or on the Rand and McNally Map of Massachusetts.

Although each of these has what might be called a lakelike expansion just back from the sea, some of them, as for instance, Barnstable, Nauset, and Chatham Harbors, can hardly be said to have rivers flowing into or through them. Hampton, Parker, Essex, Mashpee, and Slocums Rivers are in tidal marshes and the expansions in them are due mainly to coastal bars or islands. The last two are in low, sandy country. The first 5 might perhaps be in sight of mountains, but of the 10 only the Merrimack seems to have the high land nearby called for in the relations. Newburyport, which is on the south bank, is on fairly high ground. Farther up, on the same side of the river, is a hill more than 40 feet high, and still farther up, opposite Carr Island, is one 120 feet high. This lies in a bend of the river. The channel into the Merrimack is given a maximum depth over the bar of 16½ feet, as noted above, but this is modified by the statement of the Coast Pilot Guide and it is not indicated what it might have been before the jetties were constructed. The river enters the sea between two offshore beach islands, back of which and between them and the present Newburyport is a shallow expansion known as Joppa Flats. The mean high tide at the mouth of the river is 8 feet and at Newburyport 7.8 feet, and the lowest tide to be expected in either place is 3.5 feet. [P. 225.]

The above discussion shows that modern topography gives better warrant for locating Hop at the mouth of the Merrimack than in Mount Hope Bay with its two deep entrances and four rivers, or the shallow Back Bay. Nevertheless, I do not present the Merrimack as the site of Hop and the center of Wineland. The entrance seems to be too deep and the lakelike expansion too shallow, nor have I allowed for changes in the coast line due to the sinking of the land, changes produced by ocean currents, and so on. It is merely the best prospect that came out from an examination of coast charts. Further investigation might make the case for it stronger or weaker. For the present I would merely remark that it is as good as any other theory involving the New England coast.

A different region entirely was, however, suggested by Gustav Storm many years ago. This was Nova Scotia and, although the outer coasts of Nova Scotia do not have harbors suggestive of Hop, that is not the case with those in Northumberland Strait. Indeed, the southern shores of the Gulf of St. Lawrence in the provinces of Nova Scotia and New Brunswick, and the north shore of Prince Edward Island present features similar to those of southern New England and those indicated as surroundings of Hop.

On the northern coast of Prince Edward Island there are two principal entrances to consider, Malpeque Bay and Cascumpeque Bay, the former with 12 feet over the bar and 5-7 fathoms inside; the latter with 5 feet over the bar and 10 feet in Cascumpeque Harbor (U. S. Hydrographic Office, St. Lawrence Pilot, 1924, pp. 179 seq., and 183). The streams flowing into these, however, are hardly of the size called for, the mountains are wanting, and it is unlikely that navigators sailing south along the New Brunswick coast would have shifted their course to Prince Edward Island without mentioning the fact.

On the mainland from east to west we find the following inlets with their soundings as given in the St. Lawrence Pilot (pp. 83-128, 187-198):

Merigomish Harbor, N. S., 14 feet over the bar but with an intricate channel.
Pictou River, N. S., 19 feet over the bar at low water; inside 5-7 fathoms.
Pugwash Road, N. S., 6 feet over Lewis Bar; "Pugwash River, immediately within the harbor, extends into a small lake, 1½ miles long and 1 mile broad, with 2¼ to 6 fathoms at low water."
Cocagne Harbor, N. B., 10 feet over the bar; 2¼ to 4 fathoms inside.

Buctouche River, N. B., 7 feet over the bar; inside channel wide with depth of 2-3 fathoms.

Miramichi Bay, N. B., 1 or 2 feet over the bar in most places but 22 feet in the ship channel which has been dredged.

Pictou Harbor would seem to be excluded from consideration on account of the depth of water at its entrance, but a case might be made out for any one of the others.

The argument as between New England and the Nova Scotia-New Brunswick coast must turn largely upon descriptions of the climate and the presence of grapes. In 1910 the botanist Fernald put forth a theory that the term in the Sagas translated grapes really referred to cranberries (*Vaccinium vitis-idæa*) or to a species of currant, and that the Norse did not get south of Labrador. His contention, however, was rather successfully countered 3 years later by A. L. Andrews and has not been accepted by most of the commentators on the Norse voyages (Fernald, 1910, pp. 17-38; Andrews, 1913, pp. 28-36). Whether there was anyone in Karlsefni's party who had ever seen grapes or not, I am satisfied that neither cranberries nor currants were mistaken for them.

Wild grapes are known to have been fairly plentiful in New England, and one species (*Vitis vulpina*) extended into the valley of St. John River, New Brunswick. Another (*Vitis novae-angliae*), the Pilgrim grape, reached as far north as the valley of Penobscot River, Me. Champlain (vol. 1, pp. 323-324) first encountered grapes on Richmond Island, Me., on July 9, 1606, and records the fact as follows:

Meantime the Sieur de Monts paid a visit to an island which is very beautiful on account of what it produces, having fine oaks and nut-trees, with cleared land and abundance of vines which in their season bear fine grapes. These were the first we had seen on any of these coasts from Cape Le Have [the point in Nova Scotia where they first landed and still bearing the name]. We named it the Island of Bacchus.

The same name was given by Cartier (Biggar, 1924, p. 126) to the Isle of Orleans below Quebec, the point farthest down the St. Lawrence where grapes grew, and one of the reasons why Steensby placed Wineland in that region.

On September 21, 1606, Champlain visited Richmond Island again and found the grapes ripe (vol. 1, p. 395):

At the Island of Bacchus, we saw grapes which were ripe and fairly good, and others which were not; they had a fruit as fine as those of France, and I am convinced that if they were cultivated one could make good wine from them.

Speaking of the same event, the historian Lescarbot (1911, vol. 2, p. 323) comments thus:

At the entrance of the bay of the said district of Chouakoet is an island about half a league in circumference, on which our company made their first discovery of vines; for though they exist in places near to Port Royal, as, for example, along the St. John river, there was as yet no knowledge of them.

The Richmond Island vines are then described.

The French trader Denys, who lived in this region in the year 1645, gives testimony which is of the utmost importance. Speaking of the River St. John, particularly the lower section up to the head of navigation at the present Springhill, he says:

There is found here also a great quantity of Wild Grapes, on wild vines which bear grapes, the fruit of which is large and of very good taste; but its skin is thick and hard. It comes to maturity, and if it were cultivated and transplanted I do not doubt that it would produce very good wine. This is a sign that the cold there is not so severe, nor the snows so abundant as everyone says.

To this the editor, W. F. Ganong, appends the following footnote (Denys, 1908, p. 120):

The early English settlers on the Saint John are known to have made wine from the wild grapes, which are somewhat abundant along this river.

On the upper courses of three Nova Scotia rivers which Ganong identifies as the Allans, the Annapolis, and probably the Bear, Denys (p. 124) states that "the Grape-vine and the Butternut are also present," and he found the former on Pictou River which flows into Northumberland Strait. On this river he says (p. 190),

there are Oaks, Beeches, Maples, Black Birches, Cedars, Pines, Firs and every other kind of woods. The large river is straight in the entrance; boats go seven or eight leagues up it after which there is met a little island covered with the same woods, and with grape vines, and above which one cannot go higher towards its source except with canoes.

Later he sums up his opinion of the grapes of the region and the possibility of making wine from them (p. 203):

Let us see now whether the vine can come there to full maturity. In the first place it is certain that the country produces the vine naturally, that it bears a grape which matures to perfection, the grain being as large, perhaps, as the Muscadine. As to its juice, that is not so pleasing, since it is wild, and its skin is a little harder. But if it were transplanted and cultivated as is done in France, I do not doubt that its wine would be as good.

He planted vines on Miscou Island at the mouth of Chaleur Bay "which succeeded admirably." (P. 203.)

I know of no other references to grapes growing wild along the rivers flowing into Northumberland Strait, but if they were so "plentiful" on St. John River, one wonders if they might not at an earlier period have spread farther east in greater quantities than Denys indicates. Any idea that the climate may have altered materially is frowned upon by geologists and paleobotanists, but I do not understand that this inhibits the possibility of cyclar swings during which grapes might have spread farther east. Nor is it impossible that Indians in going to and fro along the trails from the St. John to the Gulf may have unintentionally spread grapes from one section to the other. There were several trails crossing the country in this way, one by Richibucto and Salmon Rivers to Grand Lake, and wild grapes have been found about the last mentioned in recent times. (Denys, p. 194.)

But without making such assumptions we may cite some evidence to the effect that the grapes in Wineland were not as plentiful as the narratives would indicate and that the explorers may have had to travel some distance inland to get them. If Leif came upon Wineland after crossing the entire North Atlantic as stated in the Saga, there is no certainty that his landfall was identical with that of Karlsefni, though it must have been well to the south. All that we learn from it is that specimens of grape vines were carried to Greenland by Leif. Nothing is said as to their abundance. This is indeed implied in one place in the narrative of Karlsefni in the words "wherever there was hilly ground, there were vines," but this party is not said to have carried grapes back to Greenland. Moreover, the two stories that have come down to us which profess to describe how grapes were discovered imply that they were at some distance from the place where the Norse had settled. The one included in the Saga attributes the find to two Scottish slaves who had been presented to Leif by King Olaf and loaned Karlsefni for this expedition. They were directed to run south and return by the end of the third half day which they did, bringing specimens of self-sown wheat and grapes. To be sure this episode is placed at Streamfirth, but it has long been recognized that it is an interpolation and it is generally held that it applies to the time when they reached Wineland proper. According to the story in the Flat Island Book, grapes were discovered by a German named Tyrker who had advanced farther into the country than his companions. The Flat Island Book is also mainly responsible for the supposed abundance of grapes. Excepting in the note above quoted there is no evidence for that in the Saga, and the specimen of grapes carried back by Leif is the only mention in it of any "cargo" of this fruit. It is possible that there is just enough truth in Nansen's myth theory to enable us to suppose that the "self-sown wheat" and grapes were noted because they fell in line with existing conceptions of the Islands of the Blest and what ought to be found there, and that may also have been why the name Wineland was applied to the country. The spirit of the reporter long antedated the newspaper.

In brief, it is possible that grapes were found only in the interior of the new country and did not occur in such quantities as we have been led to suppose.

That this south shore of the Gulf of St. Lawrence may have seemed to travelers from Greenland an earthly paradise is illustrated by the fact that a name of similar significance was given by Denys to one river flowing into the Gulf. He called it "the River of Cocagne," which, says his editor, "means . . . . a land of the greatest abundance, and has something of the significance of the English Utopia." But listen to Denys himself (pp. 192-193) :

I have named this river the River of Cocagne, because I found there so much with which to make good cheer during the eight days in which bad weather obliged me to remain there. All my people were so surfeited with game and fish that they wished no more, whether Wild Geese, Ducks, Teal, Plover, Snipe large and small, Pigeons, Hares, Partridges, young Partridges, Salmon, Trout, Mackerel, Smelt, Oysters, and other kinds of good fish. All that I can tell you of it is this, that our dogs lay beside the meat and the fish, so much were they satiated with it. The country there is as pleasing as is the good cheer.

The editor comments in a footnote (p. 192) that except for an error in distance (which does not appear in the part above quoted) Denys' description "is accurate and appreciative."

Another favored spot was Miramichi River. On the lower part of it were great quantities of strawberries and raspberries, great numbers of pigeons came there to feed, and salmon passing over the flats made such a noise that the explorers could not sleep. It is not surprising to be told, therefore, that it was a favorite resort of the Indians (p. 199).

What is said of Wineland weather is less favorable to the St. Lawrence region. The best authorities are agreed that the length of the day as given in the Flat Island Book would allow for an identification with any region up to 49° N. latitude. Therefore that item helps little. The same document goes to the absurd extreme of saying that there "was no frost in the winters, and the grass withered but little." Probably this is part of an attempt to so dress up Wineland as to make it appear a kind of earthly paradise. Both narratives affirm, however, that there was no snow, and we can hardly accept even that literally. At the same time it is a well-known fact that snowfall along the Atlantic coast is much lighter than that even a few miles inland, and remarkably open winters have been recorded at a number of points. Dr. Lewis cites the southern part of Nova Scotia and the Avalon Peninsula of Newfoundland as areas where one may look for a relatively mild winter climate. He informs me that the lowest temperature ever recorded at Yarmouth, Nova Scotia, is seven degrees below zero Fahrenheit and that only once, and adds:

On some of the Tusket Islands, off the coast of this county, and on islands off the coast of the next county, Shelburne, flocks of sheep are maintained the year around on open wild pasture, being obliged to depend entirely on their own foraging for their food and to live day and night, in fair weather or foul, without any fold, shed, or other artificial shelter. I can recall two different winters in which my father, when operating his farm on the mainland near Yarmouth, did all his plowing in the month of January, when the land was entirely free of both frost and snow.

Most of our cattle probably would not fare as well, but the stock of the Greenlanders, although housed during the winter, was no doubt accustomed to more severe weather conditions than the common run and might have stood proportionally more.

A summary of the arguments for and against a location of Wineland on the southern shore of the Gulf of St. Lawrence and the southern New England coast is now in order. Rivers with lakelike expansions corresponding sufficiently well to Hop and with offshore bars are present in both regions. Grapes grew plentifully in the latter area, and they formerly grew in parts of Nova Scotia and New Brunswick. The case for the St. Lawrence region depends on several factors—whether the Norsemen found grapes near their landing place or farther inland, and whether they were actually found in such quantities as the Flat Island Book and one expression in the Saga of Eric the Red would lead one to expect. Both regions have a winter climate rather more severe than the narratives indicate. There were parts of Nova Scotia in which winters were comparatively mild, but some of these must be excluded for topographic reasons, and it is doubtful whether similar conditions are ever matched along the south shore of Northumberland Strait. The Atlas of Canada, put out by the Canadian Department of the Interior in 1915, gives the average annual snowfall of southern New Brunswick, Prince Edward Island, and most of Nova Scotia as 60 to 90 inches (map 65), but it is evident that there is less in extreme cases. In southern New England the average number of days of snow cover during the year is between 30 on Cape Cod and along the southern coast to 90 in northeastern Massachusetts (Paullin and Wright, 1932, pl. 4). This item furnishes an argument for southern New England. In the matter of distance the northern location has the advantage. Our only clue to this is in the Saga where it is said that Karlsefni and his companions, after leaving Streamfirth, sailed southward "for a long time." The Flat Island Book which evidently confounds the Stream-firth episode with the Wineland experience would have it that they sailed from Markland for 2 dœgr, or but little more, before reaching it. If Streamfirth was the St. Lawrence estuary, and Wineland was along the southern shore of the Gulf, the distance covered was 200 to 300 miles, comparable to other distances which seem to have been covered in 2 dœgr, but if Wineland was on the coast of Massachu-setts the time consumed would have been more than three times as great. If Streamfirth is identified with the Bay of Fundy, however, the distance between it and the southern location of Wineland would have been reduced to the figures above given. From this point of view the Bay of Fundy location of Streamfirth is the more probable if Wineland was in southern New England, but on the other hand it is less probable when the time needed to reach the Bay of Fundy around Newfoundland is considered. Another argument in favor of southern New England is supplied by the account of that expedition which, according to the Flat Island Book, Thorvald's men undertook from Hop "along the western coast." A coast consisting largely of "white sands, as well as great numbers of islands and shallows" suggests southeastern Massachusetts more than any other region.

One additional statement requires some consideration, particularly as it is given in the Saga of Eric the Red. After Karlsefni's voyage to the north, on which Thorvald died and on which they "believed they had got sight of the land of the Unipeds," ended, we read:

They concluded that the mountains of Hop, and those which they had now found, formed one chain, and this appeared to be so because they were about an equal distance removed from Streamfirth, in either direction.

Juxtaposition of the three in this way has led several writers to place them near together geographically. Hermannsson, however, believes that the name Hop has been substituted for Streamfirth, and since he locates the latter in Chaleur Bay and the land of the Unipeds in the estuary of the St. Lawrence, he has no difficulty in identifying this range with the Shickshock Mountains of Gaspé Peninsula. The text, however, clearly designates *three*. Storm and Dieserud pack all these sites into Nova Scotia. But whatever may be said of the distance between Streamfirth and the land of the Unipeds, the former was much too far from Hop to be compressed into such a narrow space. Moreover, there is no reason why the voyagers should not have thought that the high lands they saw at these three places were connected even if the points of observation were far apart. It was another way of saying that they now believed they were on the shores of a continent, or at least one huge island, not in contact with a series of relatively small islands.

What is said of the inhabitants of America at this time, instead of casting light upon the places visited by Leif and Karlsefni, further mystifies us. Thus, according to the Saga of Eric the Red, the Skrellings, as they are called, arrived in skin boats, otherwise not known to have been used south of the Eskimo country except for the bull boats in the Missouri region, and they were armed with slings. As they came on they brandished "staves" and it is probable that these were spear throwers. Slings and spear throwers again suggest Eskimo rather than Indians, though this was far outside of the country known to have been occupied by the former. On the other hand, when Karlsefni went north from Streamfirth in search of Thorhall, his party encountered a Uniped who killed Thorvald with an arrow. The Flat Island Book, although it attributes Thorvald's death to an attack by a considerable body of Skrellings in canoes, confirms the fact that he was slain with an arrow and the attackers were seemingly all armed with arrows, no other weapon being mentioned. We have already raised the question whether it is possible that spear throwers were still being used in the south after bows and arrows had been adopted in the north, presumably by the Eskimo. Again, it is to be noted that, according to the Flat Island Book, the Skrellings of Hop issued out of the woods and did not come in canoes. Could it be possible that the Flat Island Book is correct in this particular, and that an attack in skin canoes which actually took place, as stated by this document, somewhere in the north has been transferred to the south by the writer of the Saga? So far as the final attack by the Skrellings is concerned, the Flat Island Book reflects Indian strategy better than the Saga. Instead of making a frontal attack, even if they had come in canoes, they would have landed at some point back of the town during the night and made an assault upon it early in the morning. The language of the Saga lends some support to the idea that this actually took place. If the Skrellings of Wineland used canoes, it is safe to infer that they were made of bark and not of skin. The Skrelling taste for red cloth is markedly

Indian, but we are puzzled to know why Karlsefni happened to have stocked his ship with it. He was, indeed, a trader, but he had had no previous experience of Indians or Eskimo. Perhaps, as one writer suggests, the sight of this red cloth roused the anger of the bull and so led to a rupture between Whites and Skrellings. Otherwise the explanation of this in the Flat Island Book to the effect that a Skrelling attempted to steal some weapon from a Norseman and was killed by him is the more probable. The writer of the Flat Island narrative has been ridiculed for speaking of the use of cows' milk in trade by the Norse, but this might have been a mere episode and not as extensive as represented, and the supplies of red cloth carried along by Karlsefni require explanation equally. The "wooden building for the shelter of grain" said to have been discovered by Thorvald's men in an island toward the west need occasion us less surprise—raised shelters of this kind being well known to the Indians —than their failure to find a single human being along coastlands which were densely occupied in later times.

It will be safe to discount the skin boats of the Hop Indians whatever we may think of those of the Unipeds, and to identify the Skrellings in that territory with the Indians, though we cannot tell whether they were the Algonquians later found in possession or not.

The "bomb" which occasioned such panic among the Norse has never been satisfactorily explained. The only suggestion made, so far as I am aware, is that of Schoolcraft, already mentioned. Unless it was some shaman's device to frighten the enemy, in which case it was eminently successful, I can suggest no explanation, and I doubt whether one ever will be suggested knowing as we do how many opportunities there were for the facts in the case to be distorted before an account was committed to writing. We may note, however, that it is given in the Saga of Eric the Red, and remark that if it had been incorporated in the narrative of the Flat Island Book it would have been regarded as another case of Flat Island Book romancing pure and simple.

The question of Norse relics need not be taken up here. The Dighton Rock, Skeleton in Armor, and old Stone Tower, in spite of a recent rehabilitation of the problem as concerns the last mentioned, may be safely rejected as valueless from the evidential point of view. The same cannot be said regarding certain more recent finds, including the Kensington Stone. But if Paul Knutson entered Minnesota and left this stone as a memorial of his visit, he came much later than Leif or Karlsefni and entered by way of Hudson Strait and Hudson

Bay. If he had previously visited and explored Wineland, we do not know where he actually went and what he called by that name. Most of the alleged Norse finds are in or near the St. Lawrence drainage area and if authenticated would merely confirm what we have independent reason to believe.[8]

SUMMARY OF CONCLUSIONS

A few general conclusions may now be ventured.

First, sound opinion identifies Helluland with Labrador, particularly the northern part. Exception is taken mainly by students who want to carry the Norsemen far to the south contrary to the probabilities, and are obliged to force an identification with Newfoundland.

The better scholarship is divided as to the location of Markland, one school holding it was Newfoundland though admitting that it possibly included southern Labrador, while the other believes that it was southern Labrador but possibly included northern Newfoundland.

This division of opinion is occasioned by the belief of one school that the Norse in voyaging south kept to the east of Newfoundland and the belief of another school that they entered the Gulf of St. Lawrence through the Strait of Belle Isle. The former seeks to find the Wonder-strands on the east shore of Cape Breton Island and Nova Scotia, Keelness at the northern end of the former, and Streamfirth either in the Bay of Fundy or some inlet on the outside coast of Nova Scotia toward its southern end. The other school identifies the Wonder-strands with the southern coast of Labrador and finds Streamfirth in the estuary of St. Lawrence River, Chaleur Bay, or some neighboring inlet, but is not agreed as to the location of Keelness.

There are also two theories which may be said to occupy premier positions regarding the location of Hop or Wineland. One places it in Nova Scotia or some territory immediately adjoining. The other identifies it with some point on the southern coast of New England.

For reasons already given, mainly the closer resemblance of conditions found along the south Labrador coast to the description of the Wonder-strands, I favor Steensby's theory on this point, identifying Helluland with northern Labrador, Markland with southern Labrador, and the Wonder-strands, as just stated, with part of the southern Labrador coast. I also agree with him in finding Streamfirth in the estuary of the River St. Lawrence, but differ entirely in

---

[8] This question has been very thoroughly covered by Holand (1940), but the authenticity of the Kensington Stone is still doubted by some.

the location of Wineland. As to the latter, the case for New England still seems a shade better, but there is no ground for dogmatic assertions either way.

The only original suggestions the writer has made himself are in locating Keelness at or near Cape Whittle, and in placing the land of the Unipeds and the scene of Thorvald's death in Hamilton Inlet or Sandwich Bay. My reference to the Merrimack River is hardly of the nature of a theory. The above seem to me conservative probabilities in the light of the very scanty traditions preserved to us in the Icelandic sagas.

BIBLIOGRAPHY

ANDREWS, A. LEROY.
    1913. Philological aspects of the plants of Wineland the Good. Rhodora, vol. 15, No. 170, pp. 28-35, February.

BABCOCK, WILLIAM H.
    1913. Early Norse visits to North America. Smithsonian Misc. Coll., vol. 59, No. 19.

BANCROFT, GEORGE.
    1840. History of the United States.

BARROW, J.
    1818. Chronological history of the voyages into the Arctic regions. London.

BIGGAR, H. P., editor.
    1924. The voyages of Jacques Cartier. Publ. Champlain Soc. Ottawa.

BRUNN, DANIEL.
    1918. The Icelandic colonization of Greenland and the finding of Vineland. Medd. Grønland, vol. 57. København.

CANADA DEPARTMENT OF MARINE AND FISHERIES.
    1900. The currents in the gulf of St. Lawrence. . . . , p. 5. Ottawa.

CANADA DEPARTMENT OF MINES AND RESOURCES, HYDROGRAPHIC AND MAP SERVICE.
    1941. Gulf of St. Lawrence Pilot (Canadian ed.), 2d ed. Ottawa.

CARTIER, JACQUES. (See BIGGAR, H. P.)

CHAMPLAIN, SAMUEL DE.
    1922-1936. The works of Samuel de Champlain. Edited by H. P. Biggar. 6 vols. Champlain Society, Toronto.

CURRAN, JAMES W.
    1940. Here was Vinland, a 1000 year old mystery solved. Sault Ste. Marie, Canada.

DENYS, NICOLAS.
    1908. The description and natural history of the coasts of North America (Acadia). Translated and edited by W. F. Ganong. Publ. Champlain Soc. Toronto.

DIESERUD, JUUL.
    1901. Norse discoveries in America. Bull. Amer. Geogr. Soc., vol. 33, pp. 1-18.

DUBOIS, B. H.
    1892. Did the Norse discover America? Mag. Amer. Hist., vol. 27, pp. 369-377.

FERNALD, M. L.
  1910. Notes on the plants of Wineland the Good. Rhodora, vol. 12, No.
    134, pp. 17-38.
FISCHER, J.
  1903. The discoveries of the Norsemen in America, with special reference
    to their cartographical representation. From the German by B. H.
    Soulsby. London.
FOSTER, JOHN W.
  1873. Pre-historic races of the United States of America. Chicago. (Also
    1878.)
GANONG, W. F. (See DENYS, NICOLAS.)
GATHORNE-HARDY, G. M.
  1921. The Norse discoverers of America. The Wineland sagas translated
    and discussed. Oxford.
GENTES HERBARIUM, Art. 4, Vites peculiares ad Americam Borealem, vol. 3,
    fasc. 4, pp. 232-233, 237. Ithaca, N. Y.
GOODWIN, WILLIAM B.
  1941. The truth about Leif Ericsson and the Greenland voyages. Boston.
GRANT, W. L., and BIGGAR, H. P. (See LESCARBOT, M.)
GRENFELL, W. T., et al.
  1909. Labrador, the country and the people. New York.
HERMANNSSON, HALLDÓR.
  1927. The Wineland voyages. Geogr. Rev., vol. 17, pp. 107-114.
  1936. The problem of Wineland. Islandica, vol. 25.
HOLAND, HJALMAR R.
  1940. Westward from Vinland. An account of Norse discoveries and ex-
    plorations in America, 982-1362. New York.
HORSFORD, EBEN NORTON.
  1892. The landfall of Leif Erikson, A.D. 1000, and the site of his homes
    in Vineland. Boston.
HOVGAARD, WILLIAM.
  1915. The voyages of the Norsemen to America. New York.
HOWLEY, M. F.
  1898. Vinland vindicated. Proc. and Trans. Roy. Soc. Canada, 1898, 2d
    ser., vol. 4, pp. 77-102.
JONES, CHARLES H. L., and RADDALL, THOMAS H.
  1934. The Markland sagas. (Evidently printed privately.)
JÓNSSON, FINNUR.
    (Has written extensively on various aspects of the Norse voyages for
    Norwegian publications. I know of his work only by quotations
    and comments of Steensby, Hermannsson, and others.—J.R.S.)
KOHL, J. G.
  1869. History of the discovery of Maine. Portland.
LESCARBOT, M.
  1907, 1911, 1914. History of New France, vols. 1-3. Translated and edited
    by W. L. Grant and H. P. Biggar. Publ. Champlain Soc. Toronto.
LOW, A. P.
  1896. Report on explorations in the Labrador Peninsula along the East
    Main, Koksoak, Hamilton, Manicuagan and portions of other
    rivers in 1892-93-94-95. Geol. Surv. Canada. Ottawa.

MALLET, PAUL HENRI.
 1755. Histoire de Dannemarc.
MARKHAM, C. R.
 1865. On the origin and migrations of the Greenland Eskimaux. Journ.
   Roy Geogr. Soc., vol. 35. Also in Arctic papers for expedition of
   1875.
MARKHAM, C. R., editor.
 1881. The voyages of William Baffin, 1612-1622. (In part Catonle's
   Relation.)
McLEAN, J. P.
 1892. Pre-Columbian discovery of America. Amer. Antiquarian, vol. 14,
   pp. 33-40, 87-94, 139-154, 189-196, 271-276, 316-323.
MUÑOZ, J. B.
 1793. Historia del Nuevo Mundo. Madrid.
MURRAY, HUGH.
 1829. Historical account of discoveries and travels in North America;
   including the United States, Canada, the shores of the Polar Sea,
   and the voyages in search of a north-west passage; with observa-
   tions on emigration, vols. 1 and 2. London.
NADAILLAC, MARQUIS DE.
 1883. L'Amérique préhistorique. Paris.
NANSEN, FRIDTJOF.
 1911. In northern mists. Translated by A. G. Chater.
NÓRLUND, POUL.
 1936. Viking settlers in Greenland, and their descendants during five
   hundred years. Cambridge University Press, London.
OLSON, JULIUS E.
 1906. Original narratives of the voyages of the Northmen. In Original Narratives of Early American History, vol. entitled "The Northmen,
   Columbus, and Cabot, 985-1503," pp. 1-74. New York.
PACKARD, ALPHEUS S.
 1888. Who first saw the Labrador coast? Journ. Amer. Geogr. Soc., vol.
   20, pp. 197-207.
 1891. The coast of Labrador. New York.
PAULLIN, CHARLES O., and WRIGHT, JOHN K.
 1932. Atlas of the historical geography of the United States, pl. 4.
POWER, L. C.
 1892. The whereabouts of Vinland. New England Mag., n.s., vol. 7, pp. 174-
   192. Boston.
RAFN, CARL CHRISTIAN.
 1837. Antiquitates Americanae. Copenhagen.
REEVES, A. M.
 1890. The finding of Wineland the Good. The history of the Icelandic
   discovery of America. London. (Also 1895.)
ROBERTSON, W.
 1778. History of America. London.
SCHOOLCRAFT, H. R.
 1857. History of the Indian tribes of the United States, vol. 6.
SCISCO, L. D.
 1908. The tradition of Hvitramannaland. Amer. Hist. Mag., vol. 3, pp.
   379-388, 515-524.

SMITH, J. T.
    1839. The discovery of America by the Norsemen in the Tenth Century,
        comprising translations of all the most important original narratives
        of the event; together with critical examination of their authen-
        ticity, to which is added an examination of the comparative merits
        of the Northmen and Columbus. Boston. (Also London, 1842.)
        (Map copied in Minnesota Hist. Soc. Rep.)
SOULSBY, B. H. (See Fischer, J.)
SPRENGEL, M. C.
    1782. Geschichte der Entdeck Ungen.
STEARNS, WINFRID A.
    1884. Labrador. Boston.
STEENSBY, H. P.
    1918. Norsemen's route from Greenland to Wineland. Medd. Grønland,
        vol. 56. København.
STORM, GUSTAV.
    1887. Studier over Vinlandsrejserne. Aarb. for Nord. Oldkynd. og Hist.
        København.
    1888. Studies on the Vineland voyages. English translation. Mém. Soc.
        Roy. Antiquaires du Nord. Copenhagen. (Separate, 64 pp. 1889.)
THALBITZER, W.
    1904. A phonetical study of the Eskimo language. Medd. Grönland, vol. 31.
        Copenhagen.
THÓRDARSON, MATTHIAS.
    1930. The Vinland voyages. Translated by Thorstina Jackson Walters,
        Amer. Geogr. Soc., Res. Ser. No. 18.
TORFÆUS, T.
    1706. Grölandia antiqua.
    1888. History of ancient Vinland. (Shea's translation.) Catholic Hist.
        Mag., n.s.
TWENHOFEL, W. H.
    1938. Geology and paleontology of the Mingan Islands, Quebec. Geol. Soc.
        Amer., Spec. Pap., No. 11, June 4.
UNITED STATES COAST AND GEODETIC SURVEY.
    1927. U. S. Coast Pilot, Atlantic Coast, Sect. A, St. Croix River to Cape
        Cod, 2d ed.
UNITED STATES HYDROGRAPHIC OFFICE.
    1924. St. Lawrence Pilot, Gulf and River St. Lawrence to Montreal. Publ.
        No. 100, 5th ed.
    1934. Sailing directions for the Gulf and River St. Lawrence. Publ. 100,
        6th ed.
WALLACE, W. S.
    1909. Historical introduction in "Labrador, the Country and People," by
        W. T. Grenfell et al. New York.
WATKINS, H. G.
    1930. River exploration in Labrador by canoe and dog sledge. Geogr.
        Journ., vol. 75, No. 2, February.
WEISE, ARTHUR J.
    1884. The discoveries of America to the year 1525. New York.

WHEATON, HENRY.

    1831. History of the Northmen or Danes and Normans from the earliest times to the conquest of England by William of Normandy. Philadelphia.

WILSON, DANIEL.

    1862. Prehistoric man, vols. 1 and 2. Cambridge and London.

WINSOR, JUSTIN.

    1884. Narrative and critical history of America, vol. 1. Boston.